BRAIN GAMES

Dot·to·Dot

Publications International, Ltd.

Louis Weber, CEO
Publications International, Ltd.
7373 North Cicero Avenue
Lincolnwood, Illinois 60712

ISBN-13: 978-1-4508-7575-2
ISBN-10: 1-4508-7575-0

Manufactured in China.

8 7 6 5 4 3 2 1

Connect the Dots and Engage Your Brain!

When was the last time you worked a dot-to-dot puzzle? Can't remember? Well, the puzzles you'll encounter in *Brain Games®: Dot-to-Dot* take these classic puzzles to a whole new level. Moving from one dot to the next, you'll compose wonderfully complex illustrations of all kinds of objects, places, and creatures. From detailed images of the natural world and popular sports, to intricate portraits of world destinations and common household items, you'll create them all—one dot at a time!

Just open the book to a puzzle of your choice, locate dot number 1, and start connecting! Whenever you reach a number that has a star icon instead of a dot, that means the line you've been tracing should end right there. You should then locate the next consecutive dot and start a *new* line. Some puzzles feature many of these separate lines—part of the fun is watching how they all come together in the end to form one complete image.

But the benefits of working these dot-to-dots go beyond mere entertainment. These puzzles are actually good for your mind, as well! Exercising your brain by solving puzzles can help increase your mental flexibility and build focused attention and problem-solving skills. All of these are important cognitive functions, so you can think of these puzzles as mini brain workouts.

If you're feeling especially creative, color and shading can be added to enhance each final picture. (And completed images can always be glimpsed at the back of the book, if you need a hint!) So what are you waiting for? Grab a pen or pencil, pick out a puzzle, and start connecting. With *Brain Games®: Dot-to-Dot,* you can engage your brain and have fun at the same time.

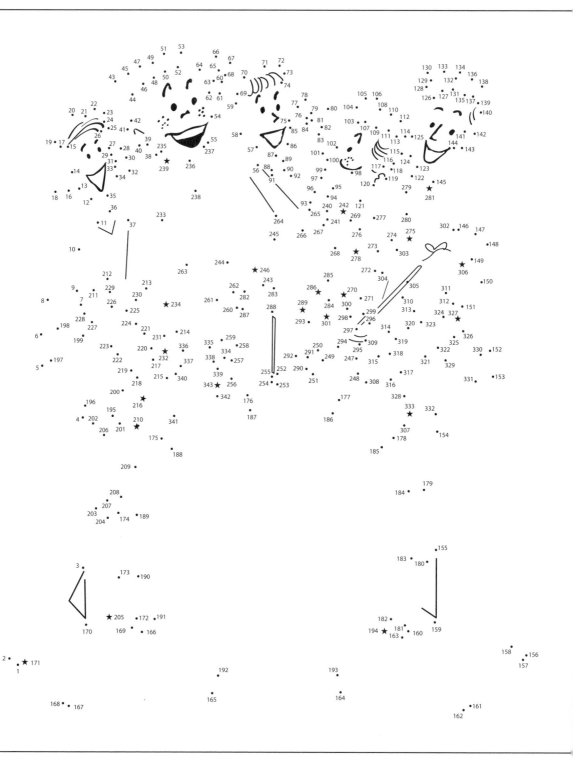

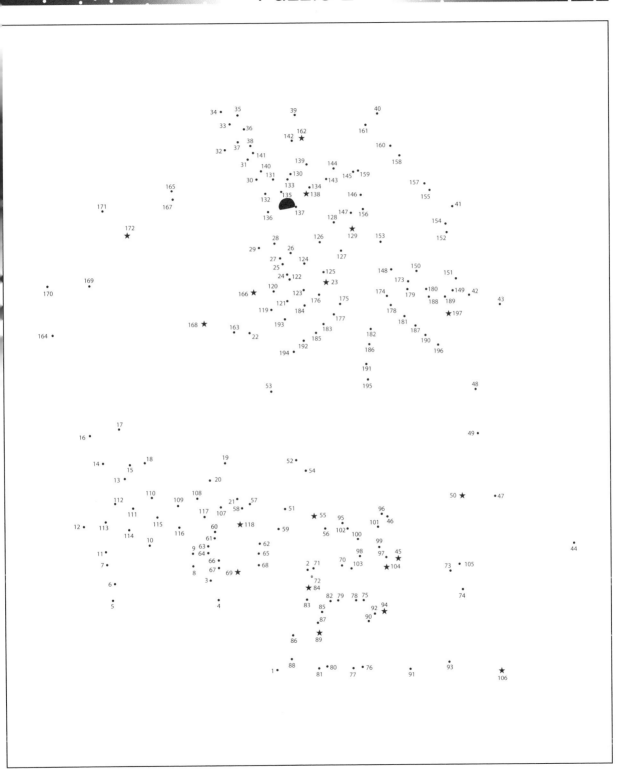

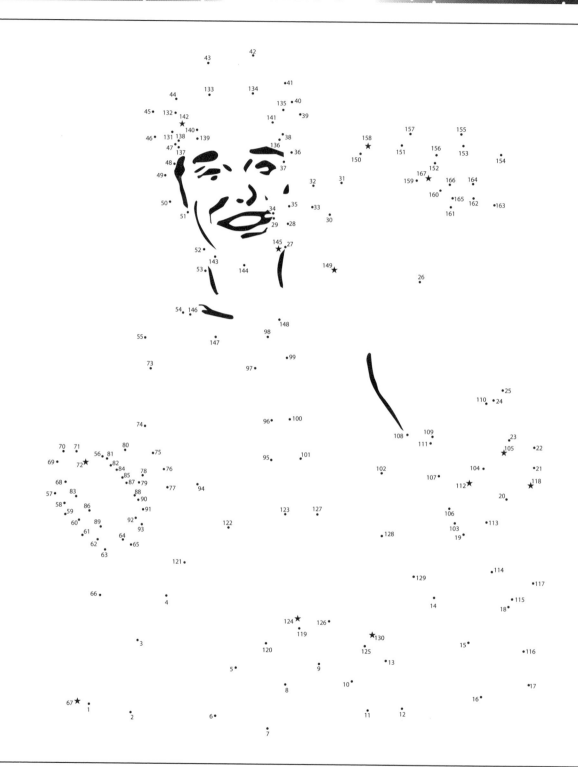

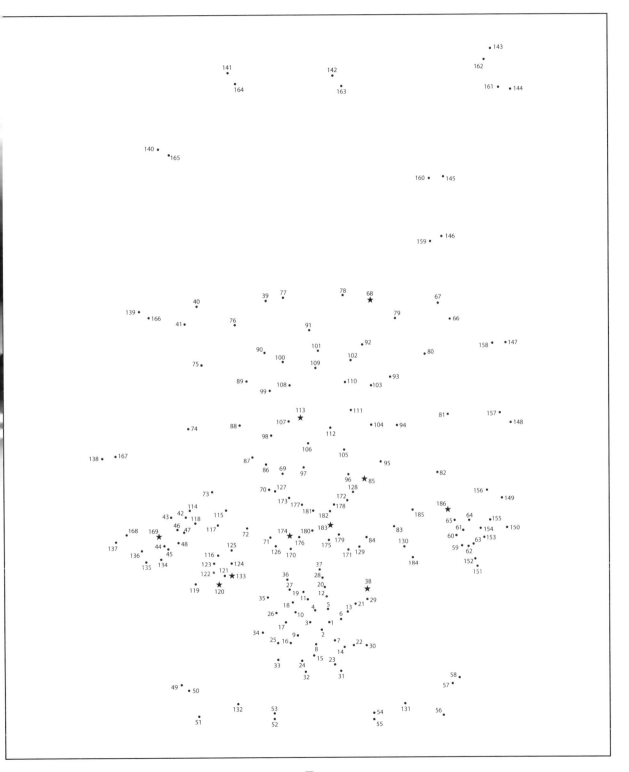

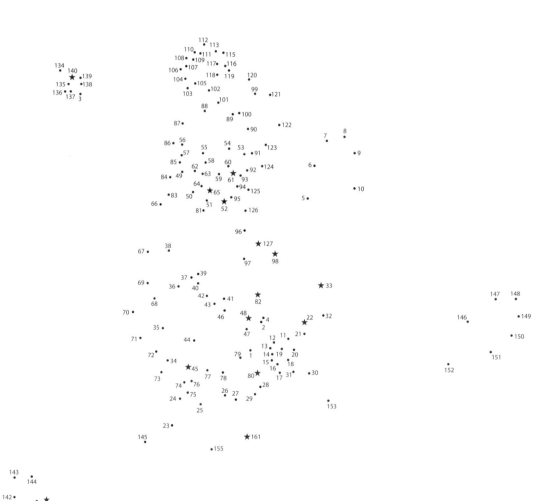

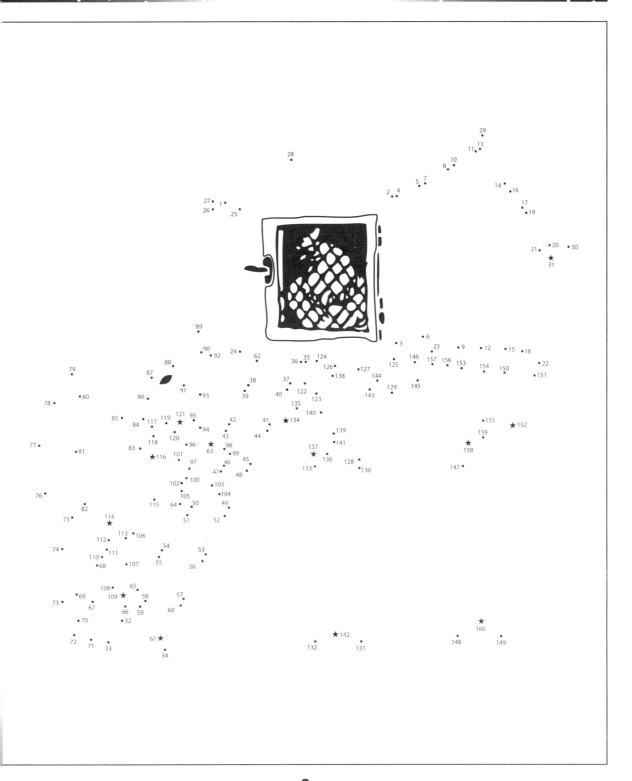

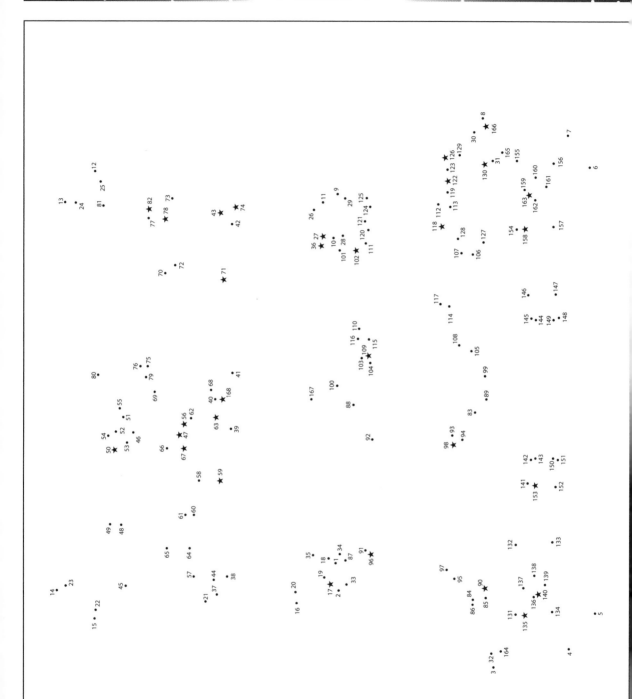

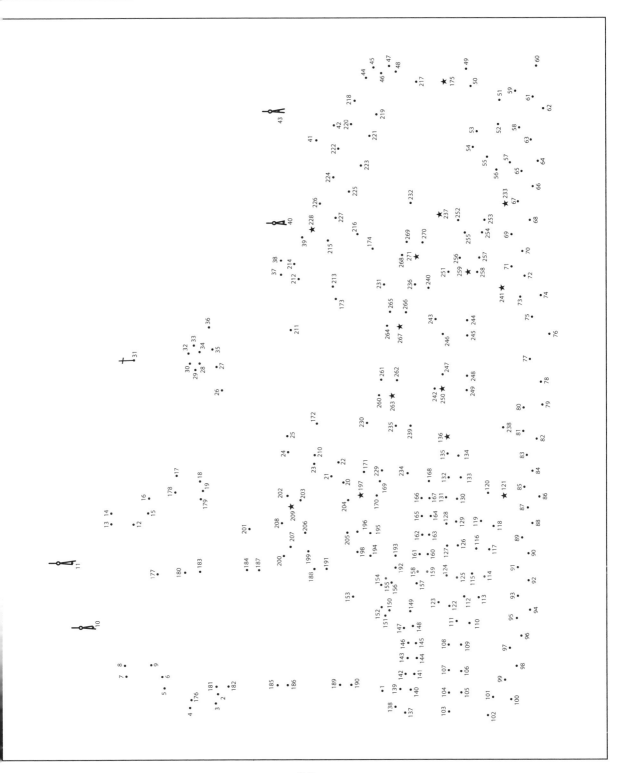

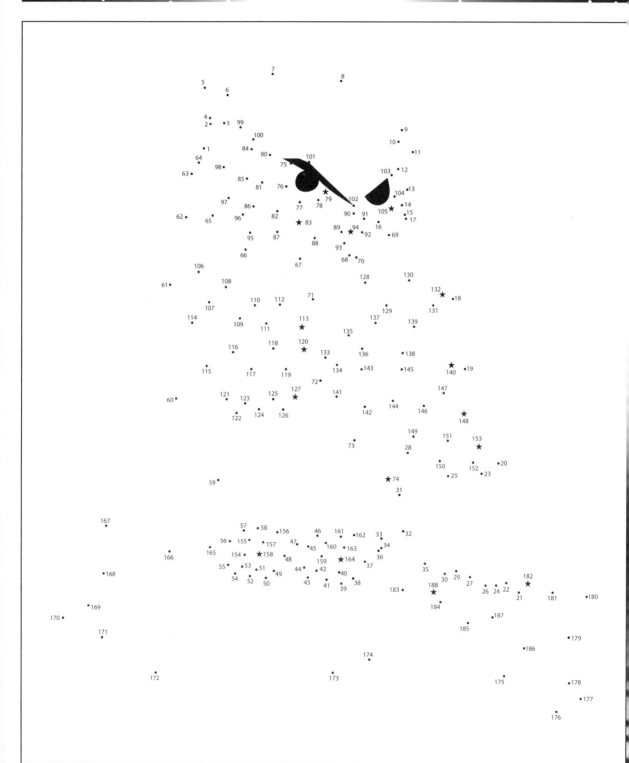

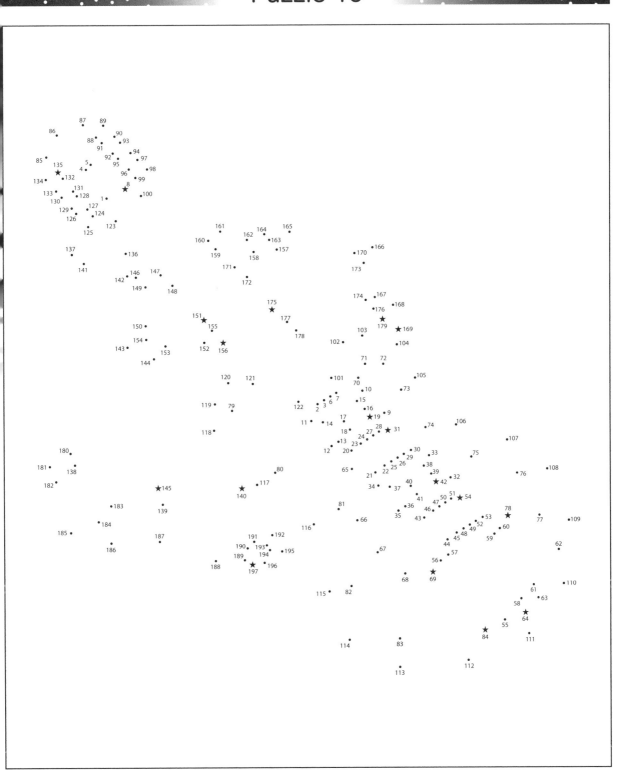

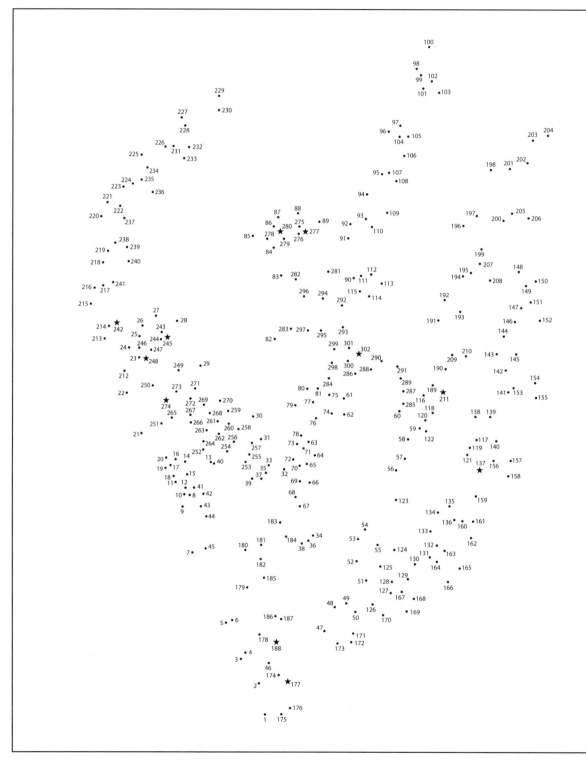

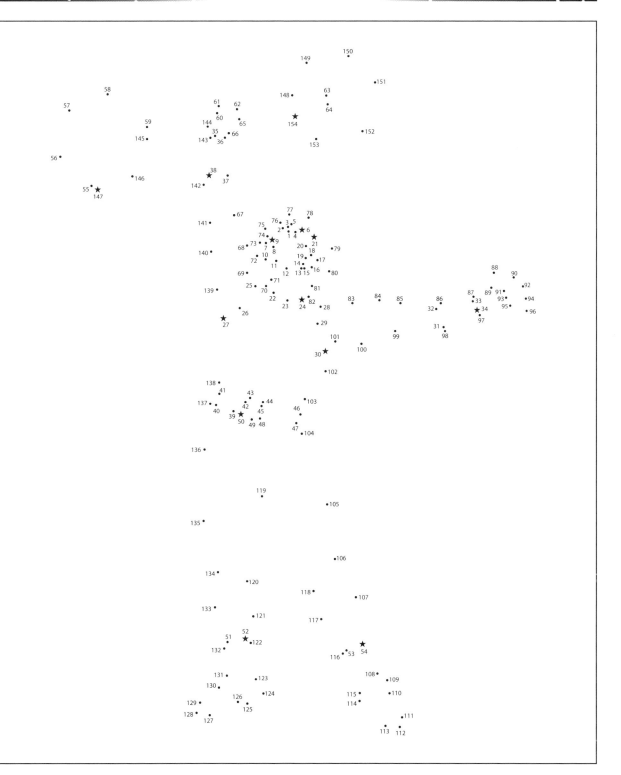

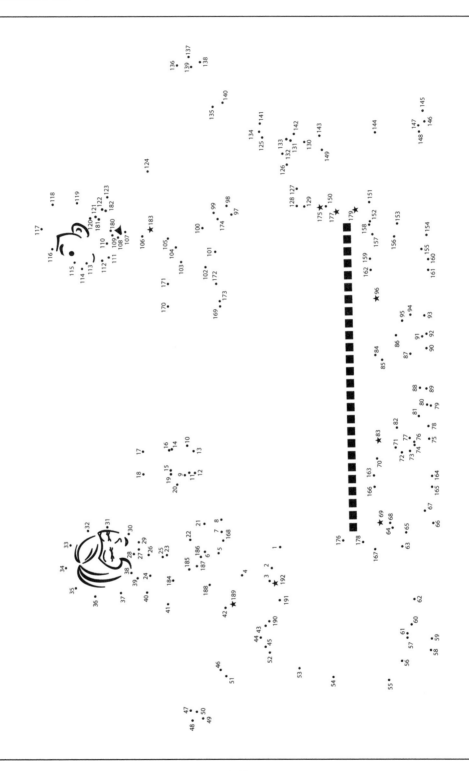

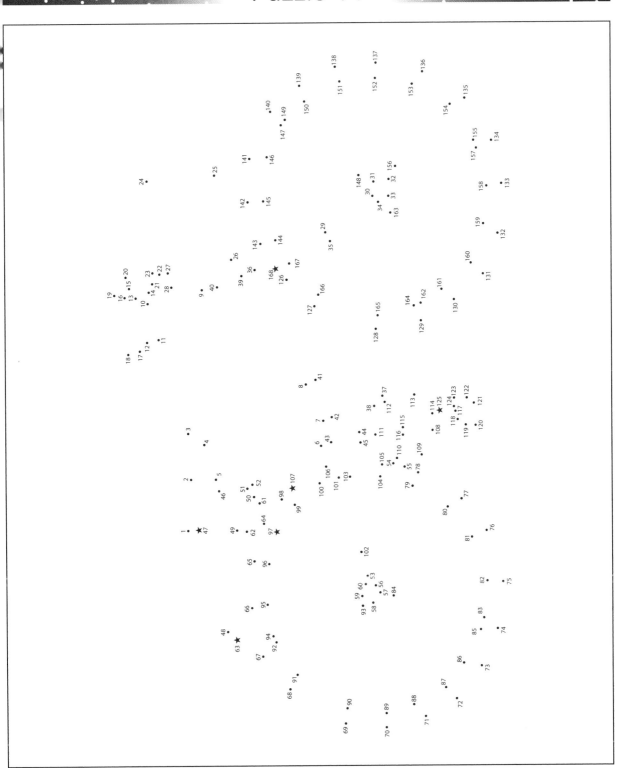

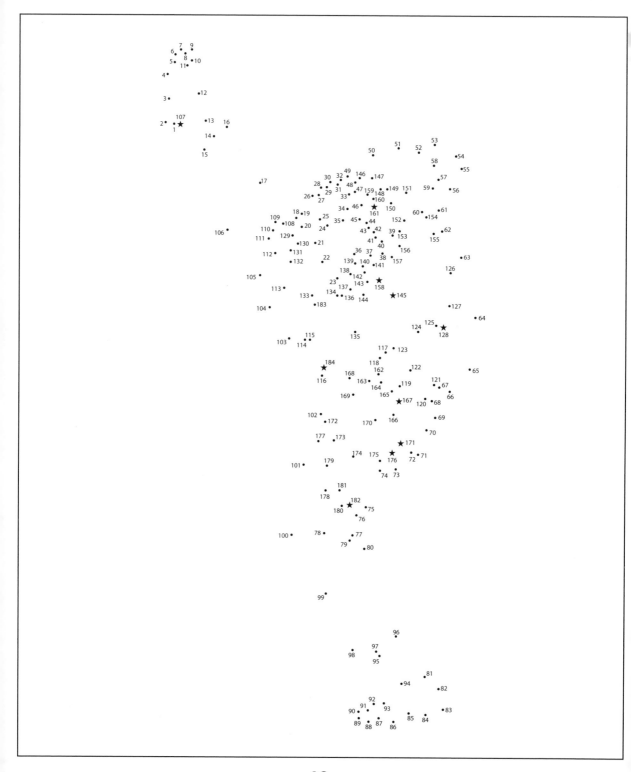

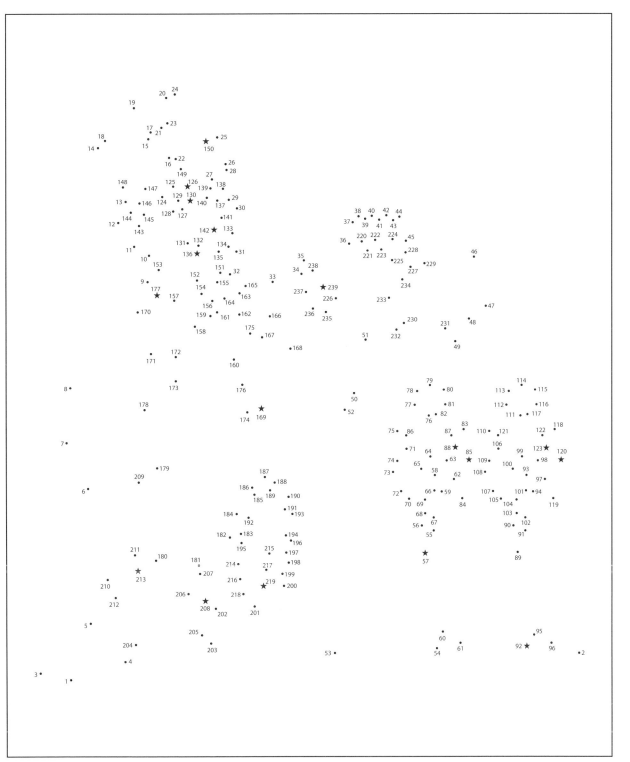

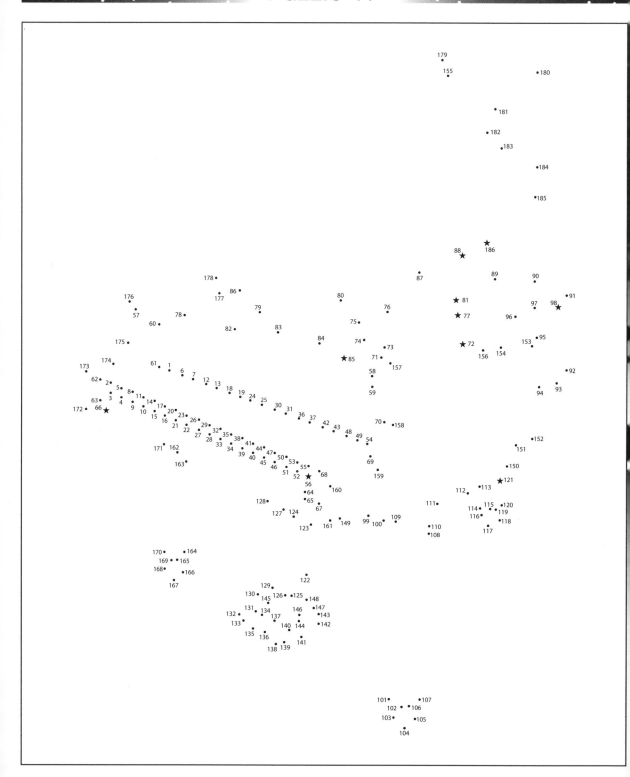

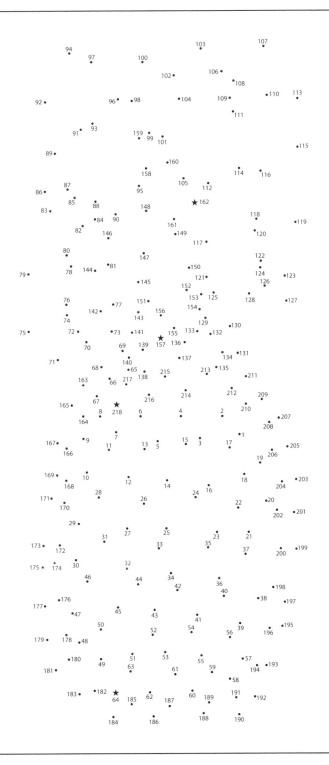

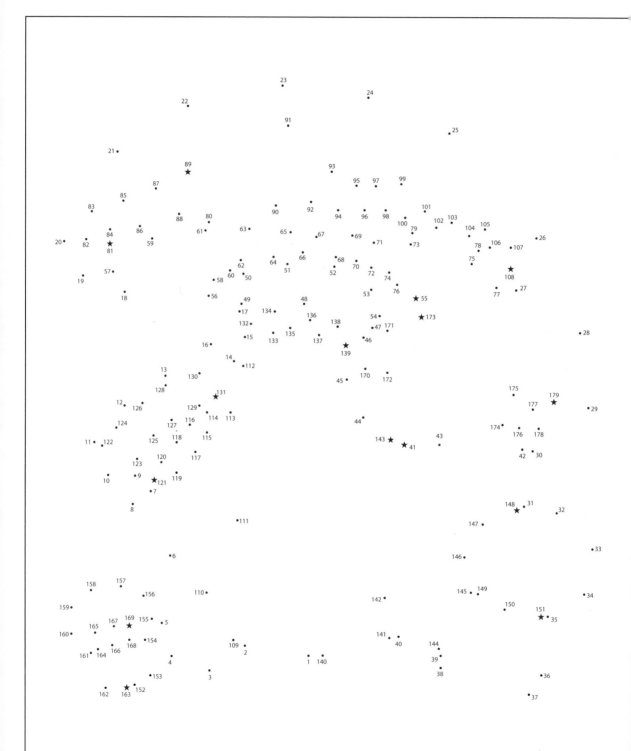

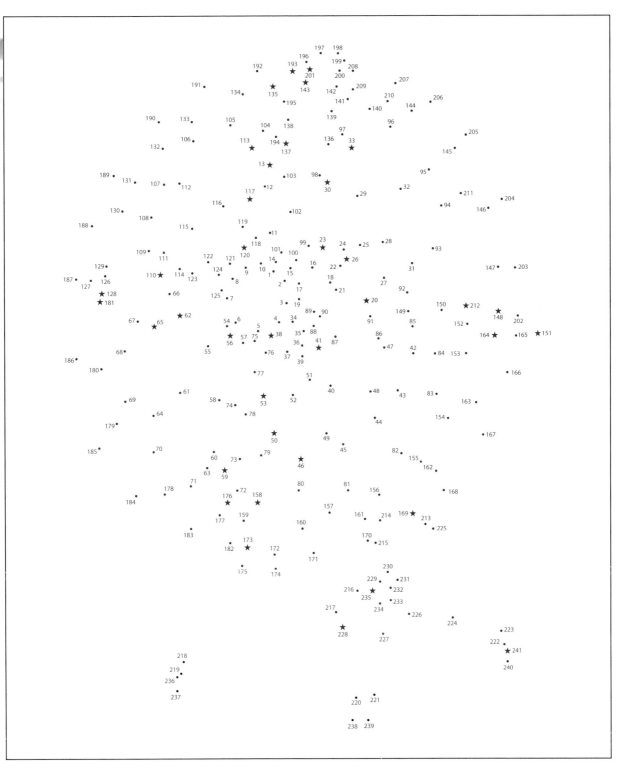

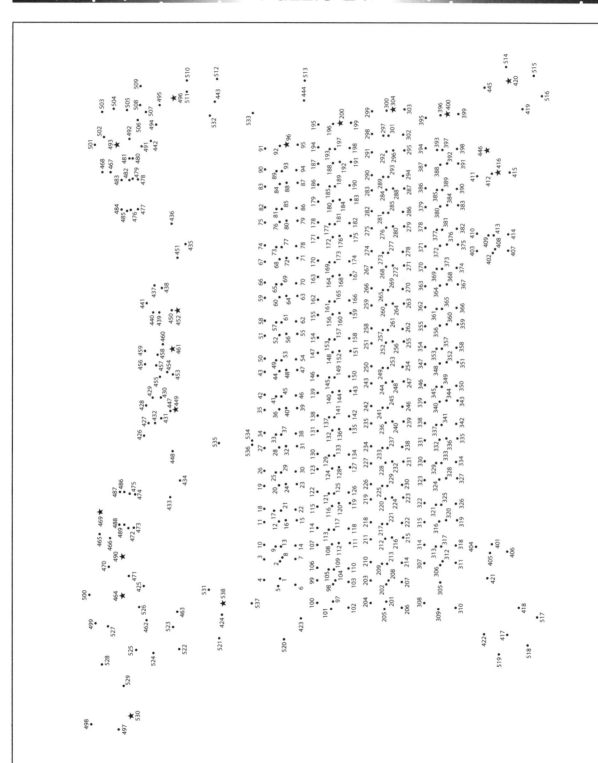

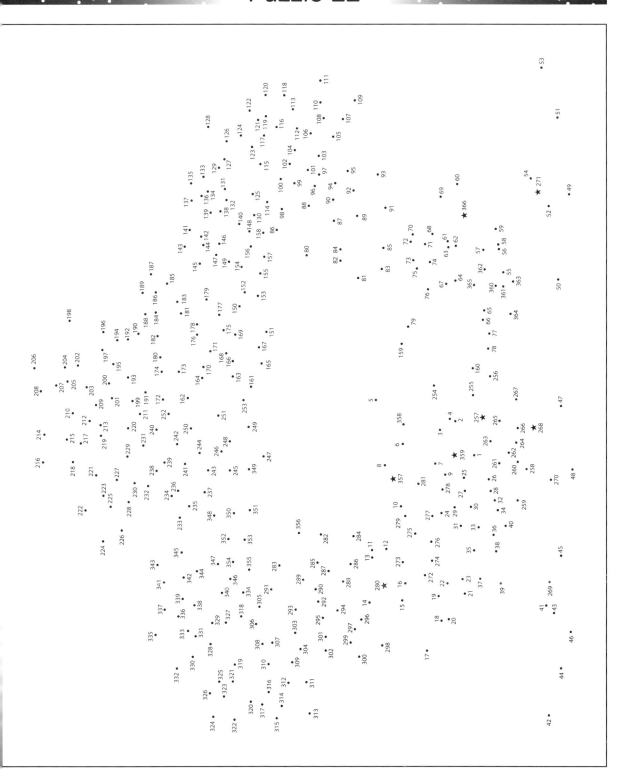

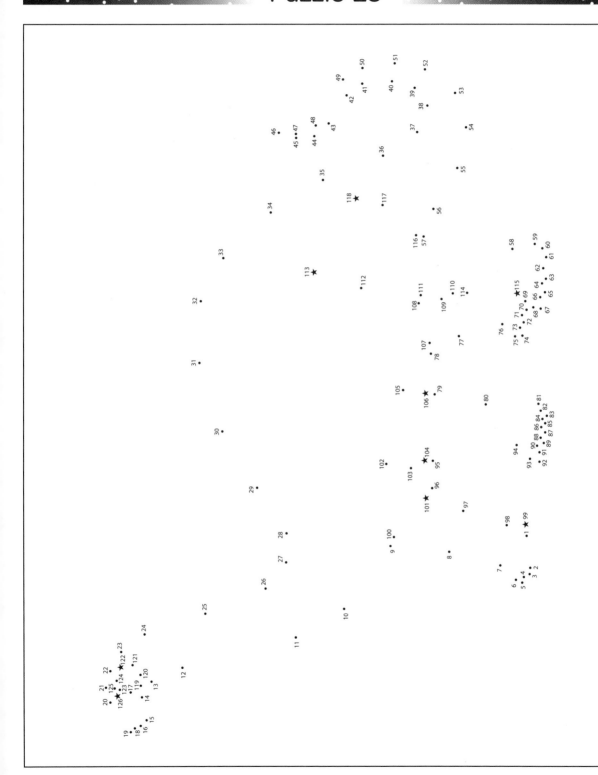

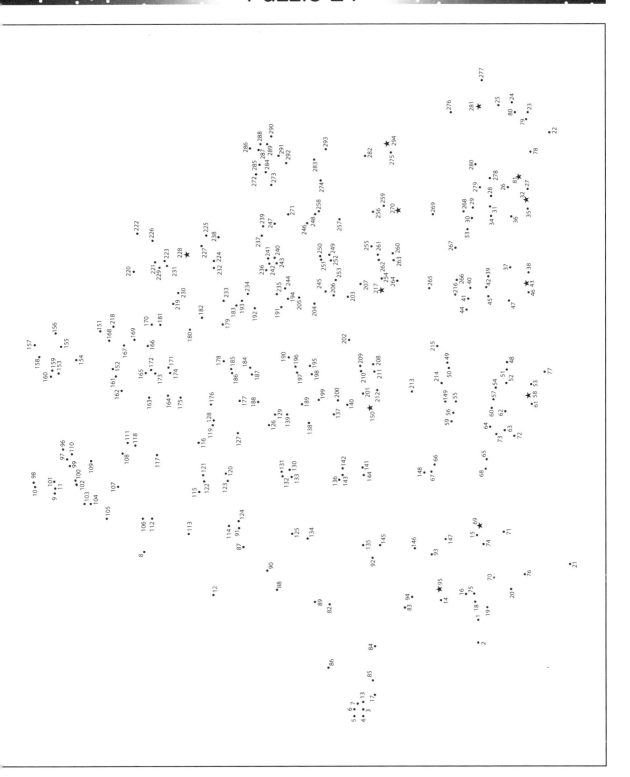

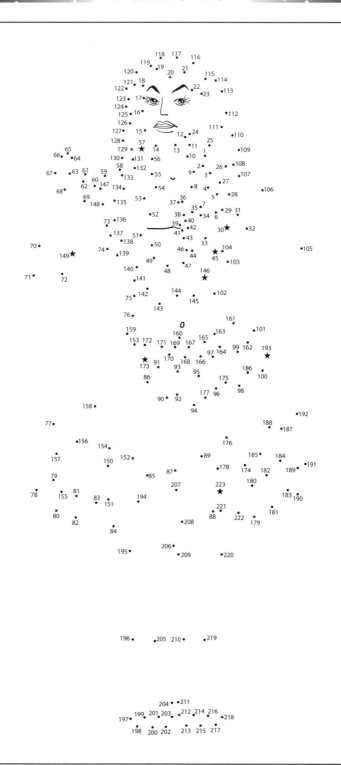

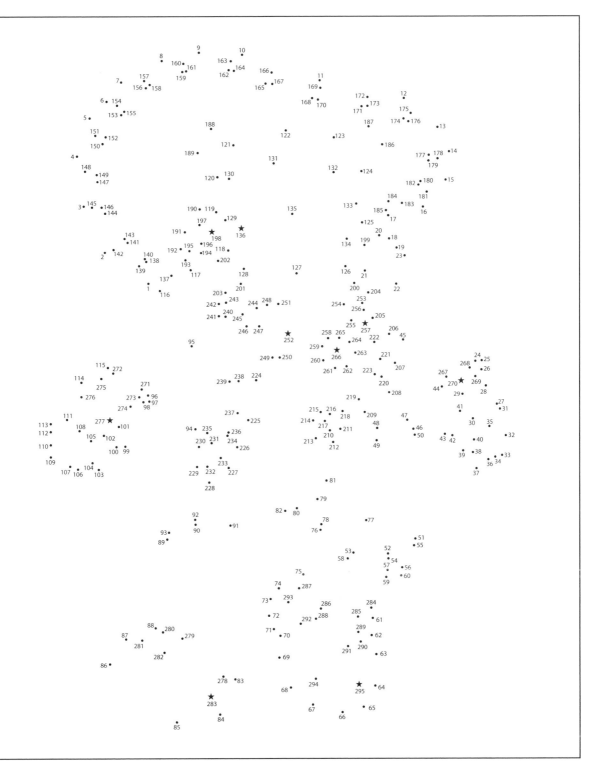

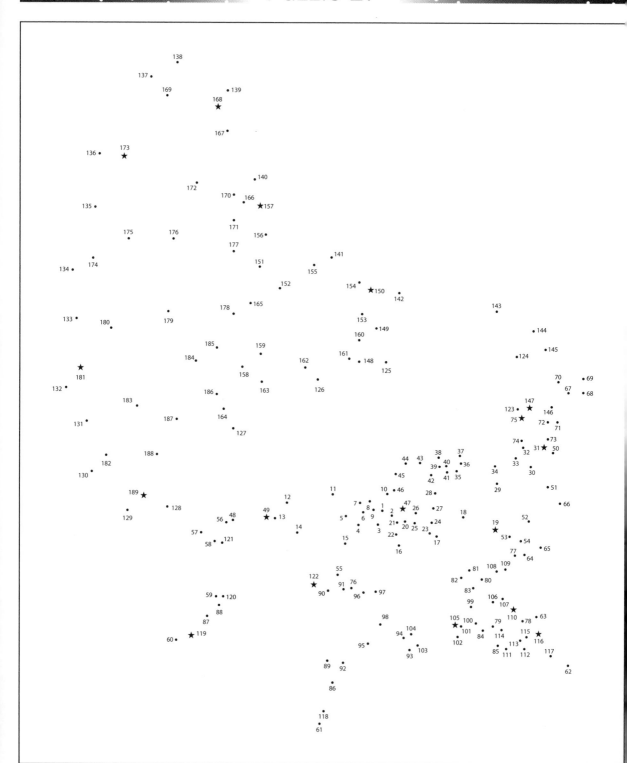

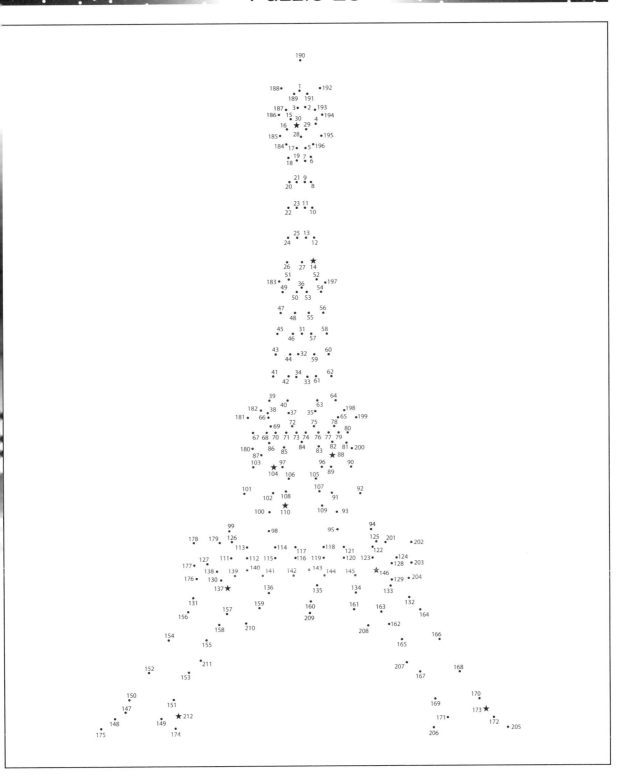

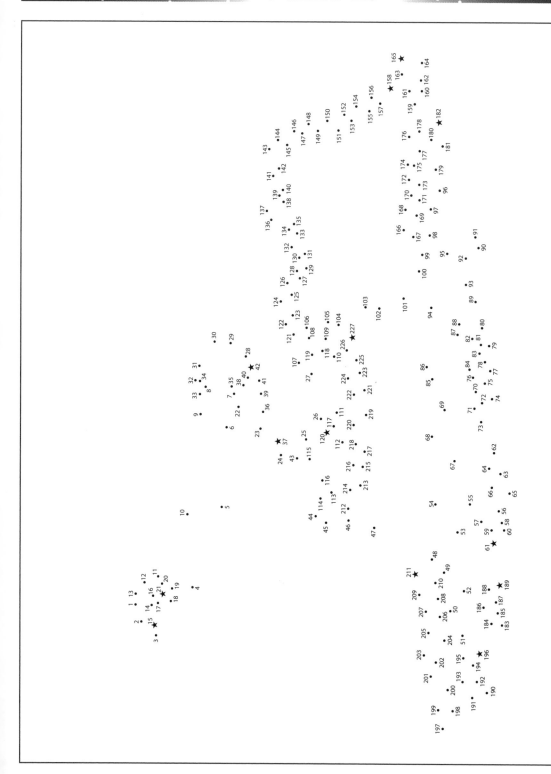

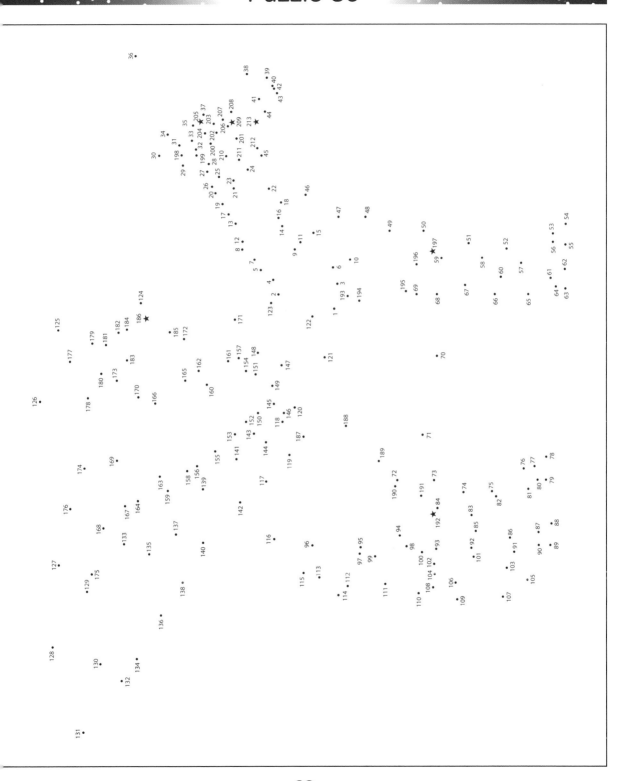

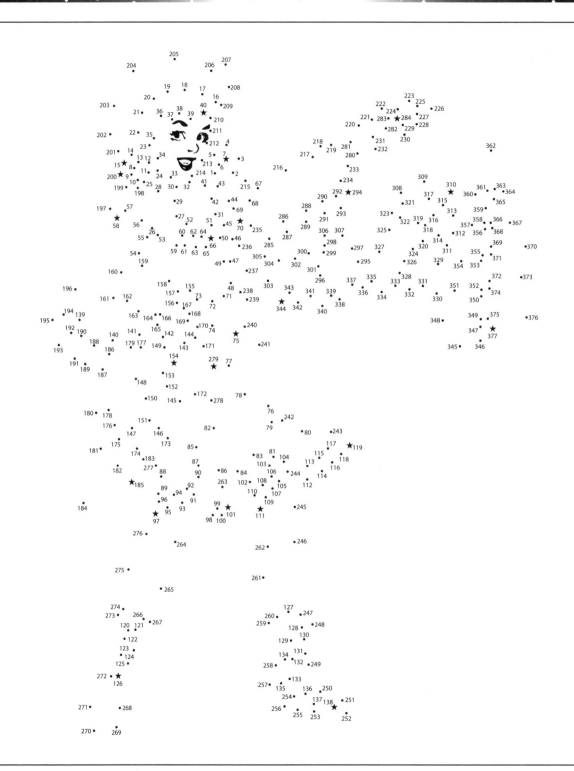

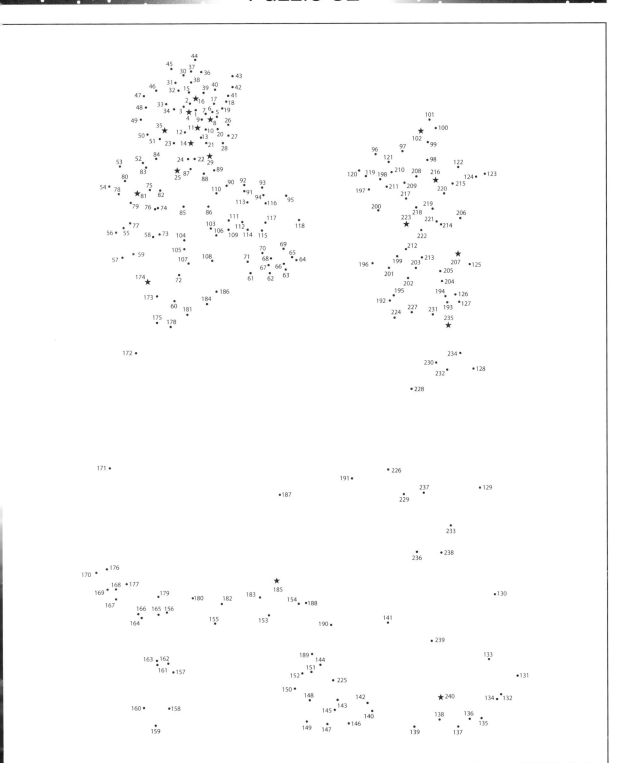

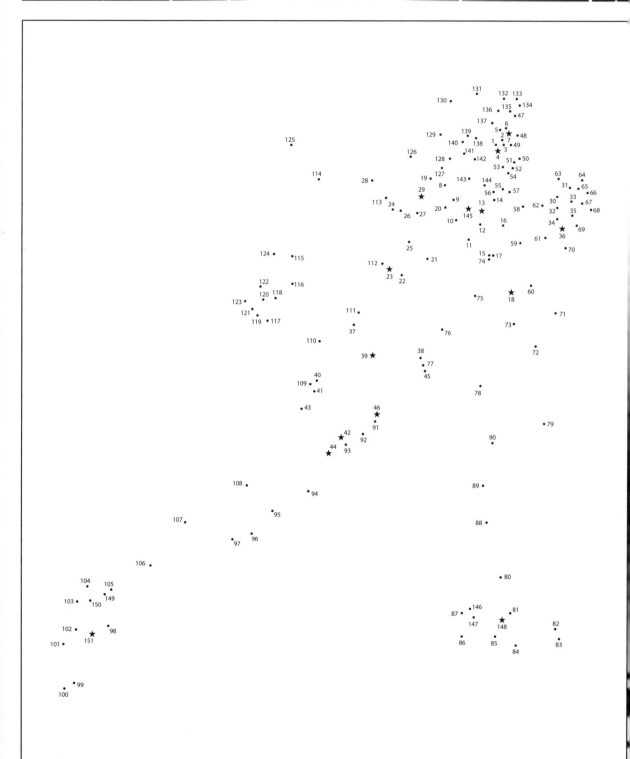

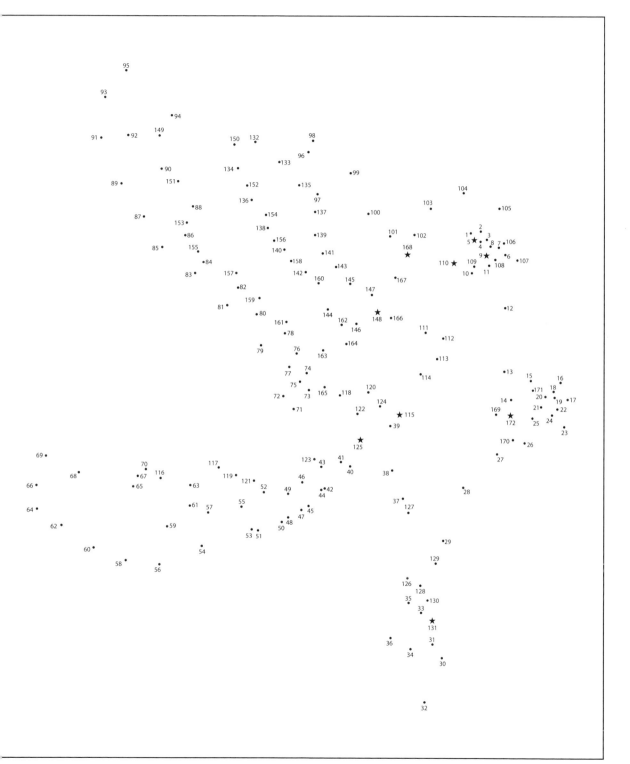

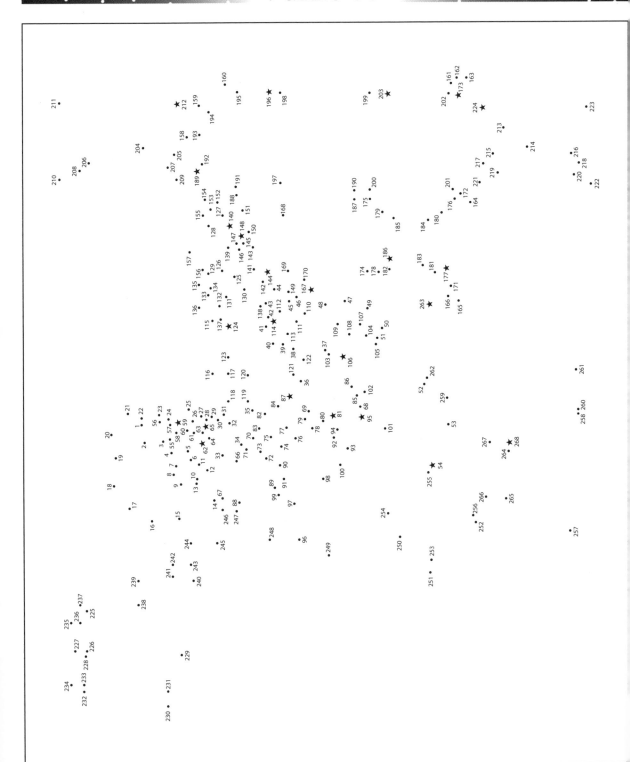

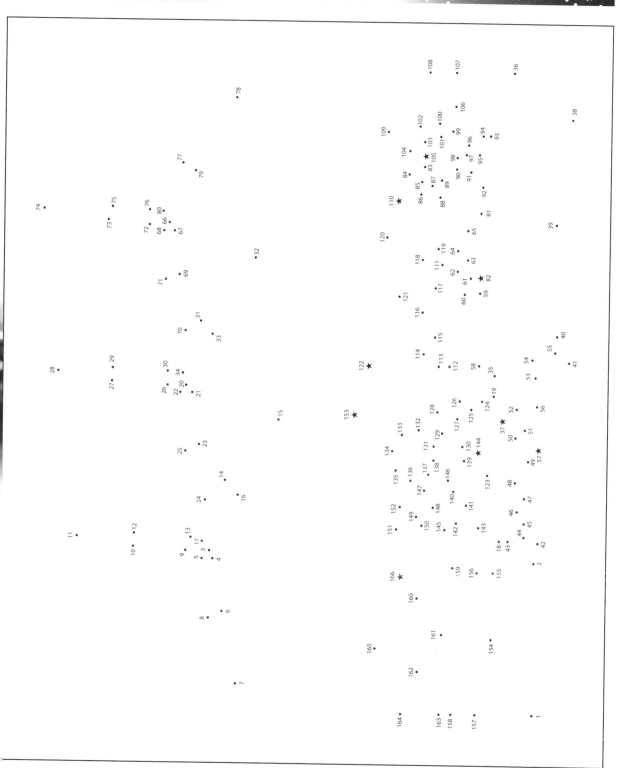

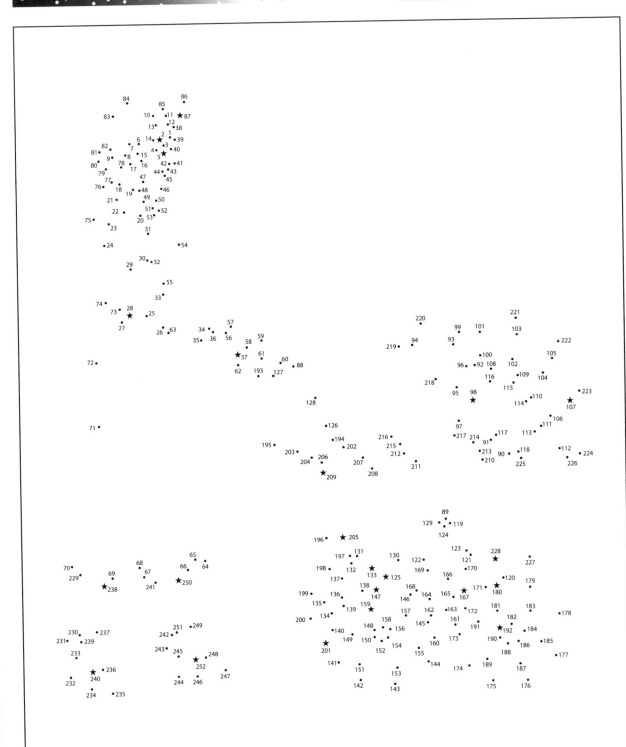

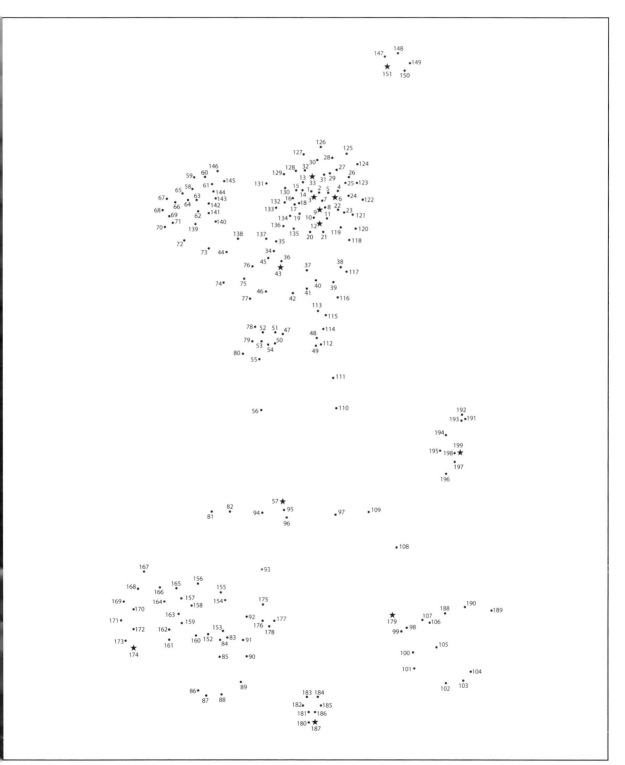

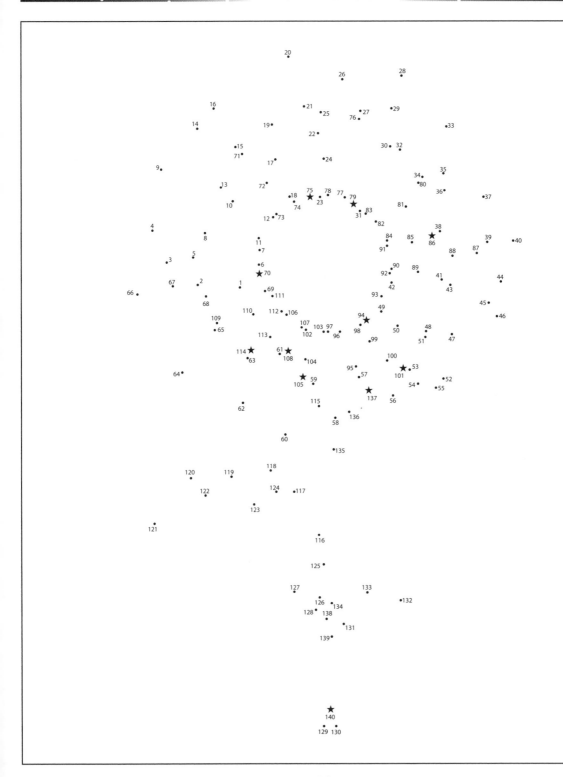

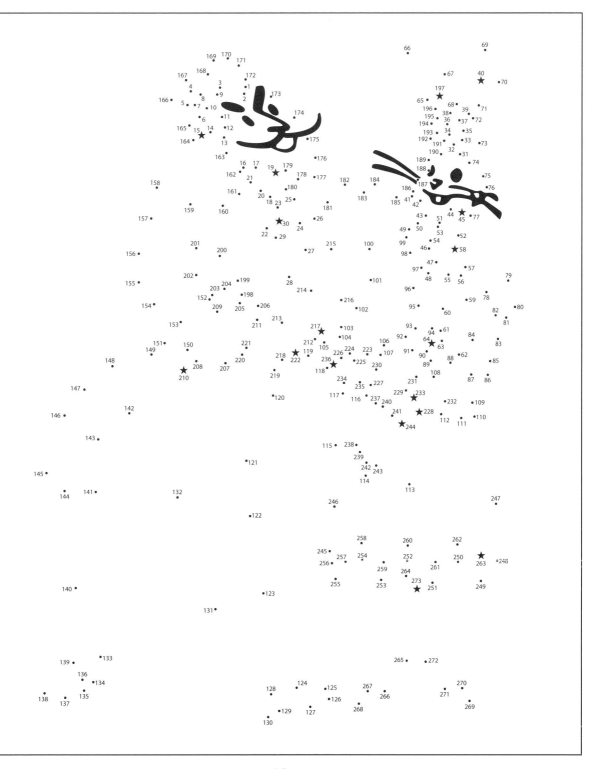

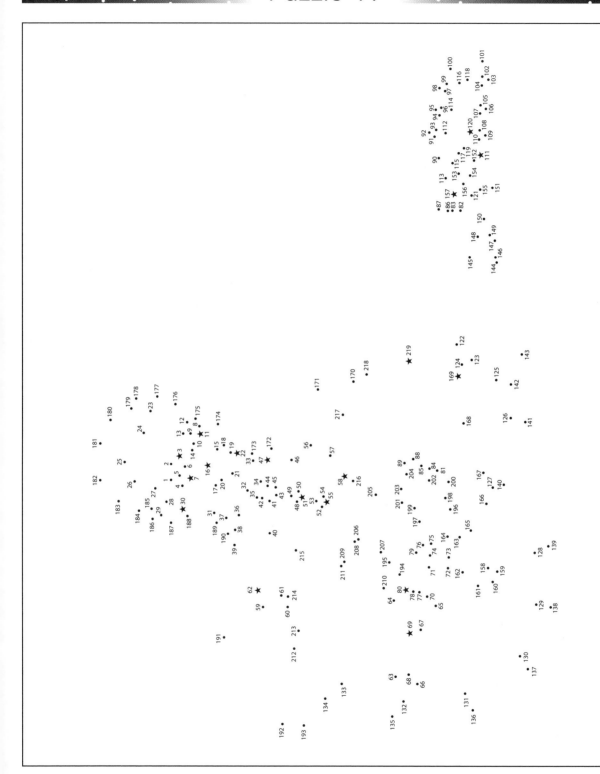

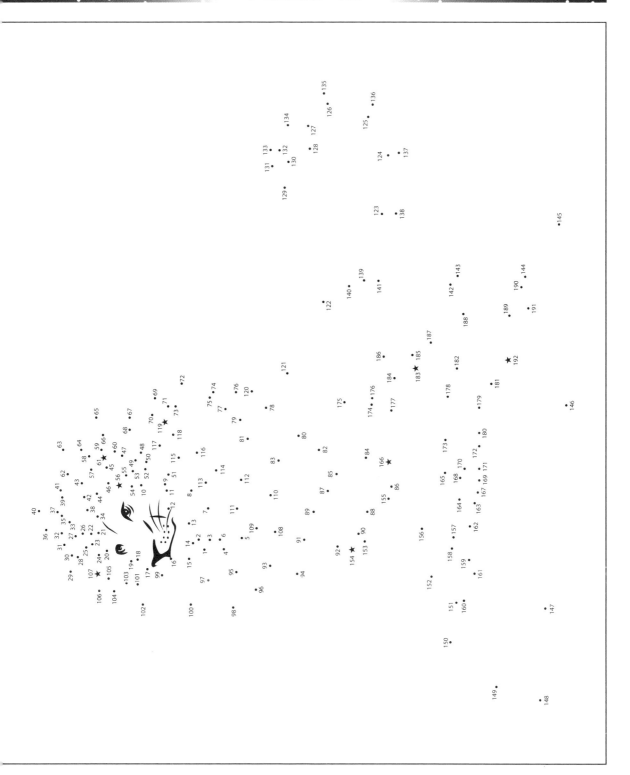

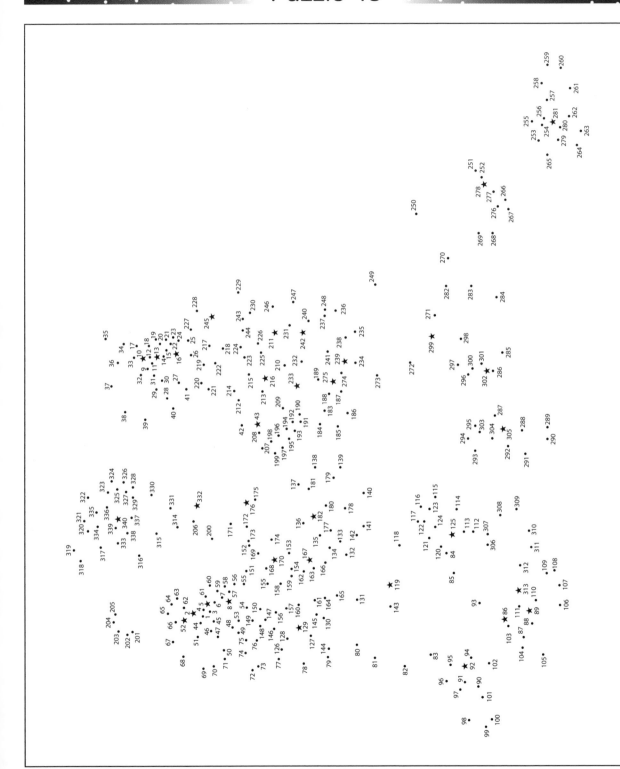

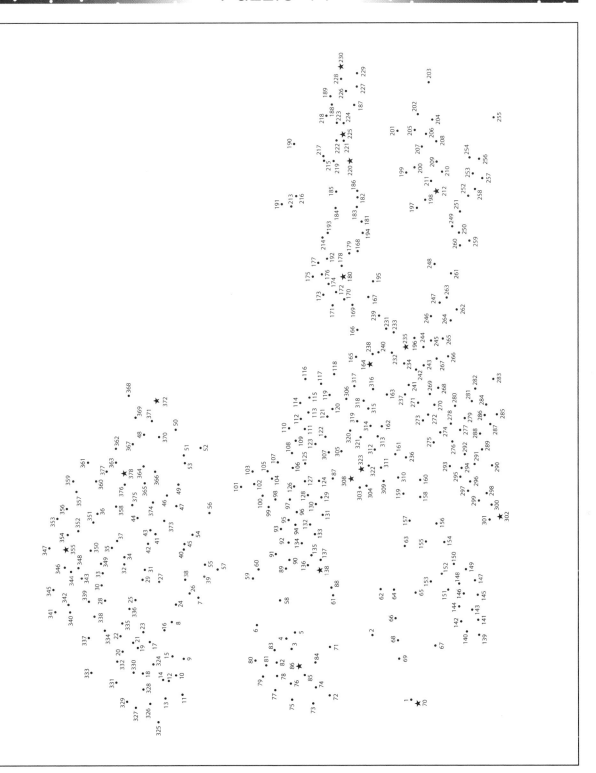

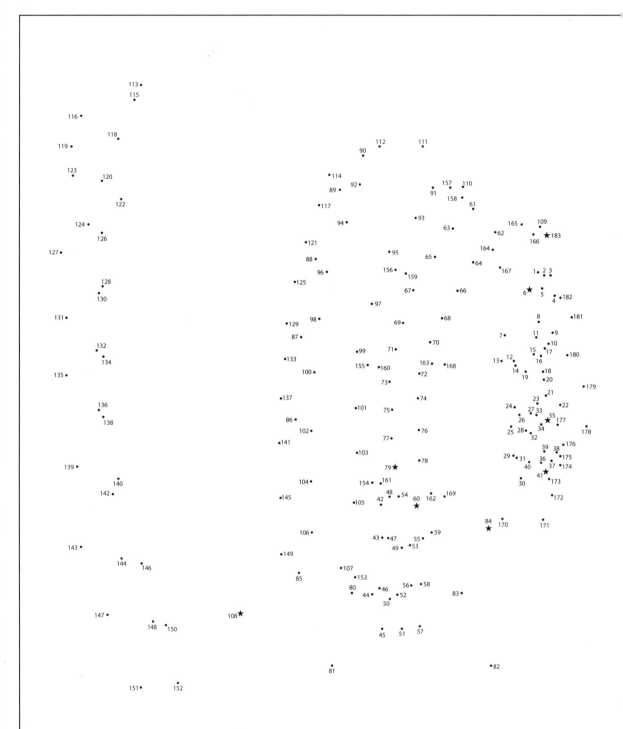

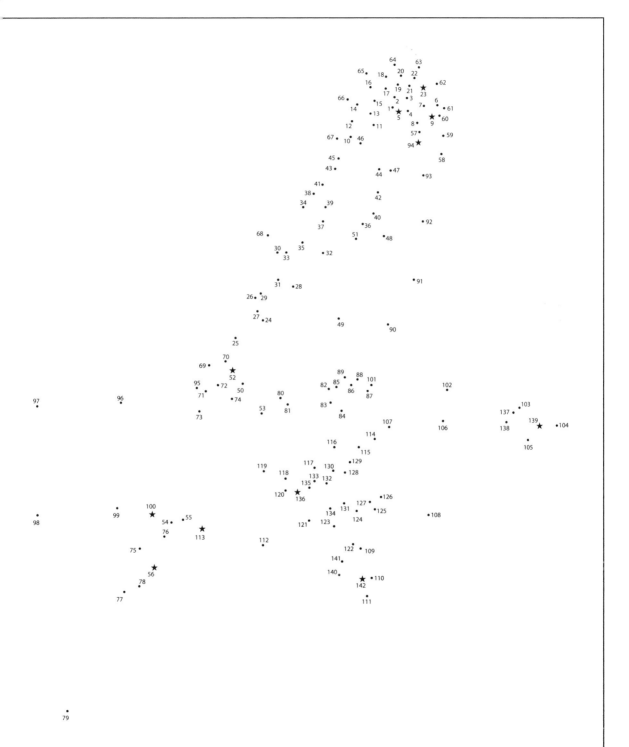

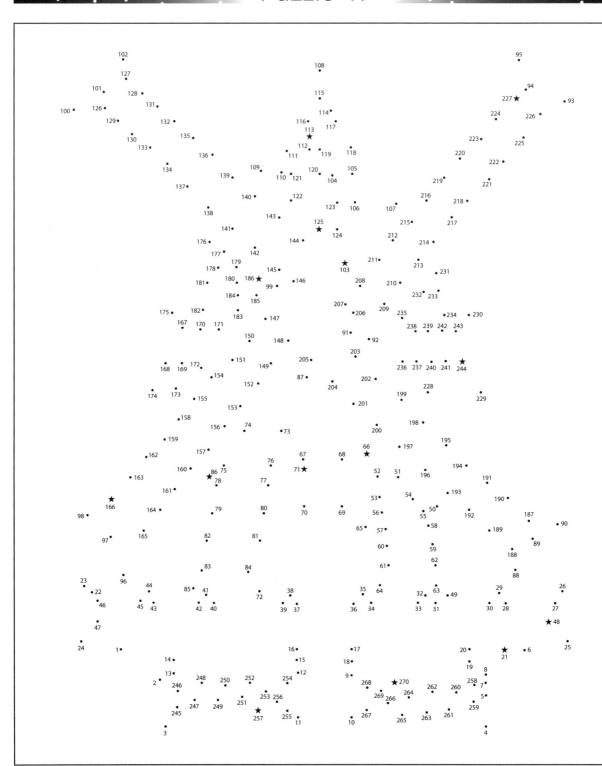

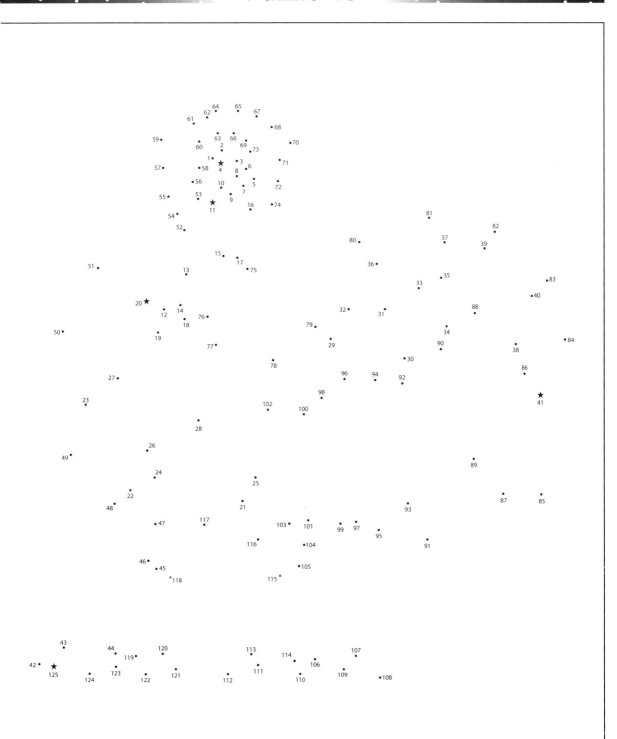

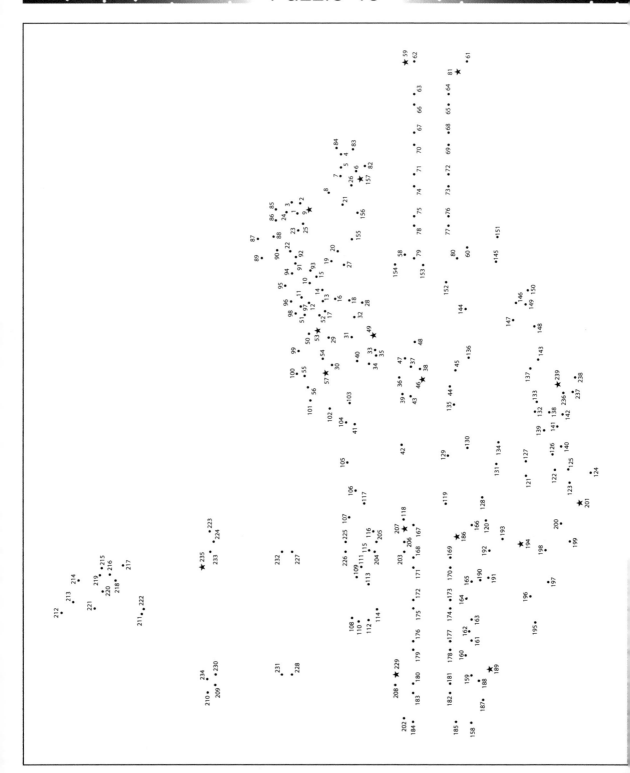

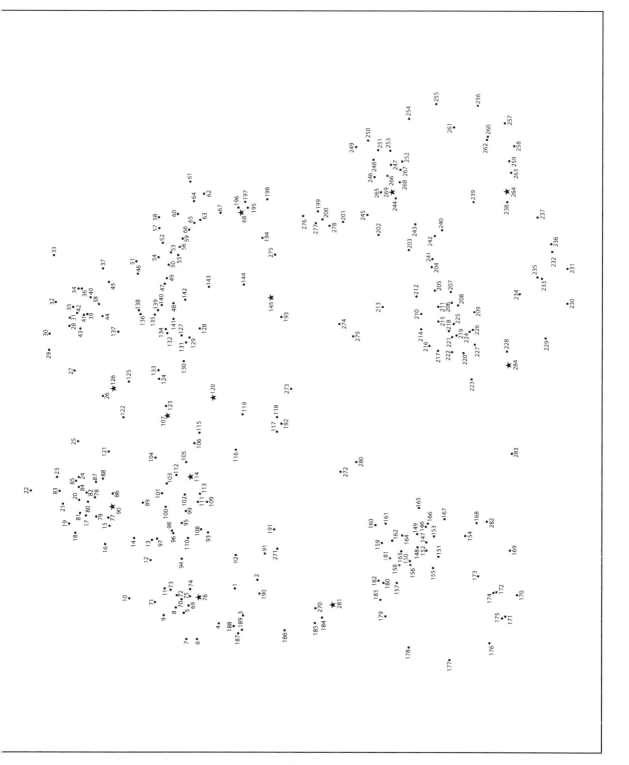

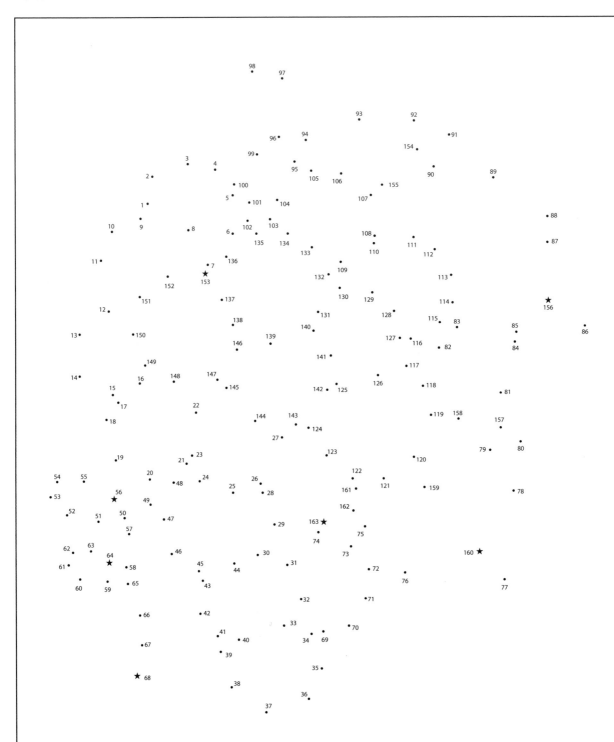

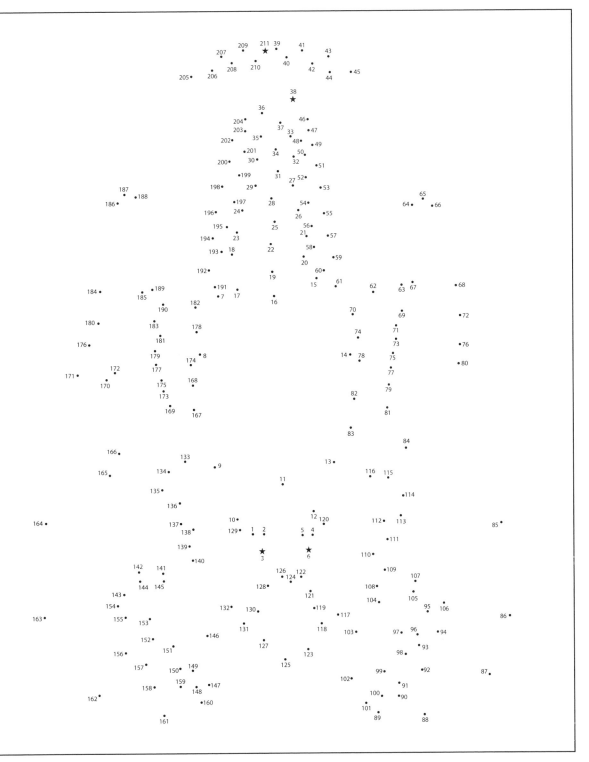

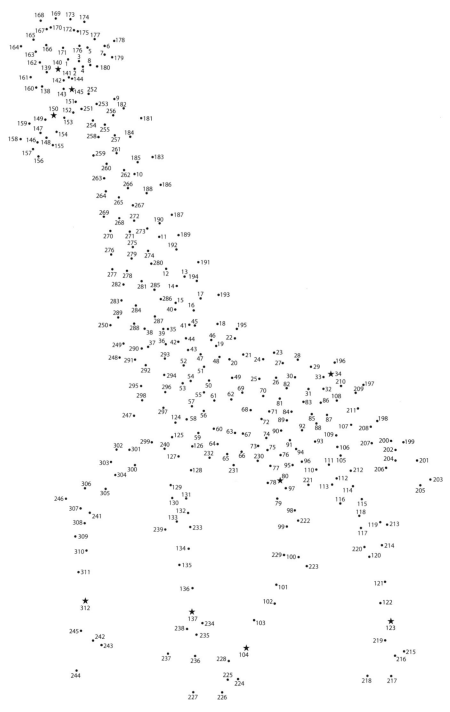

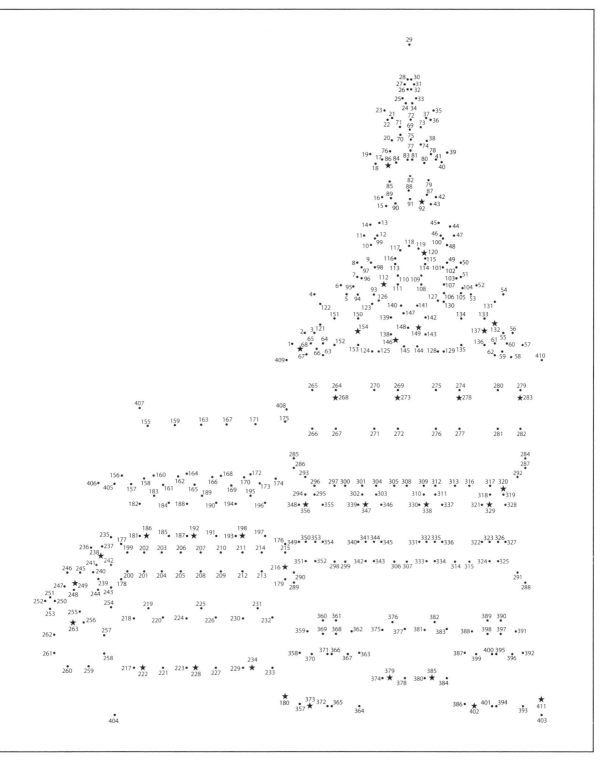

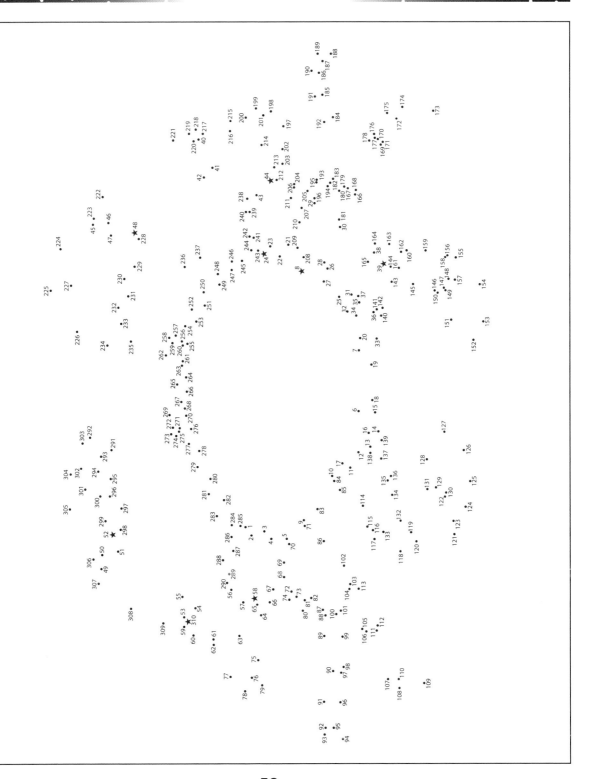

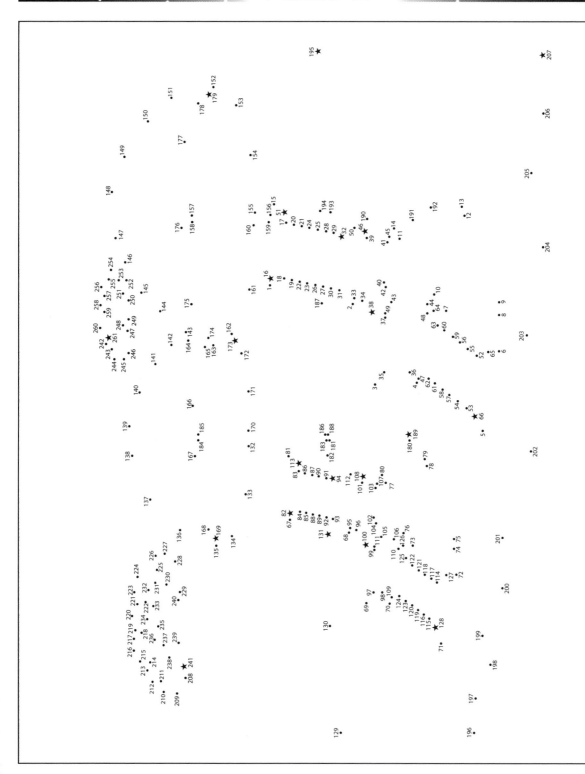

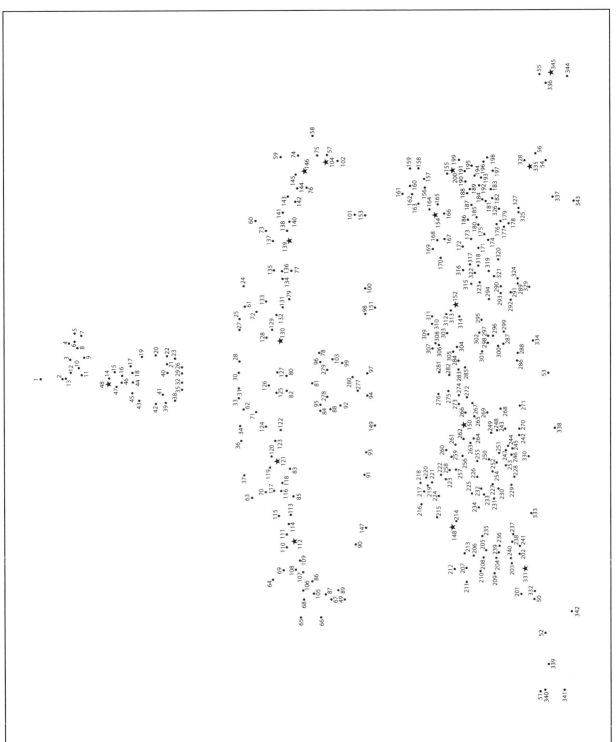

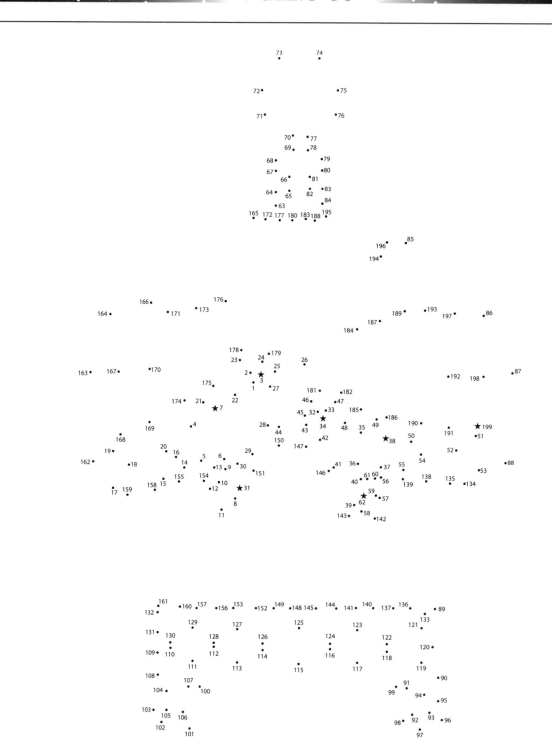

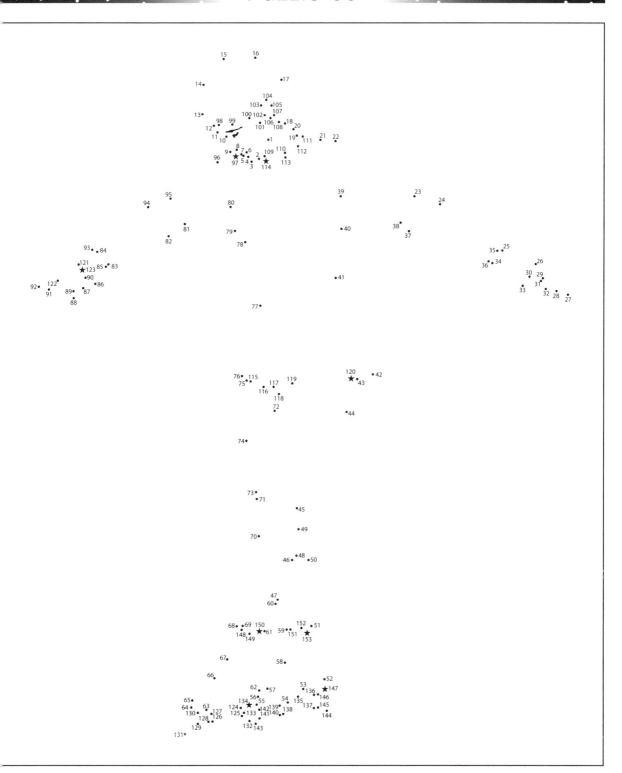

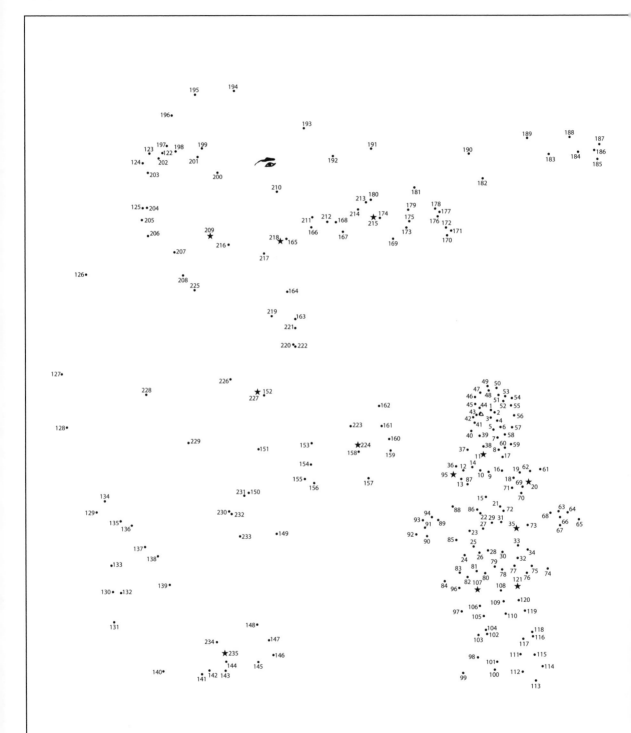

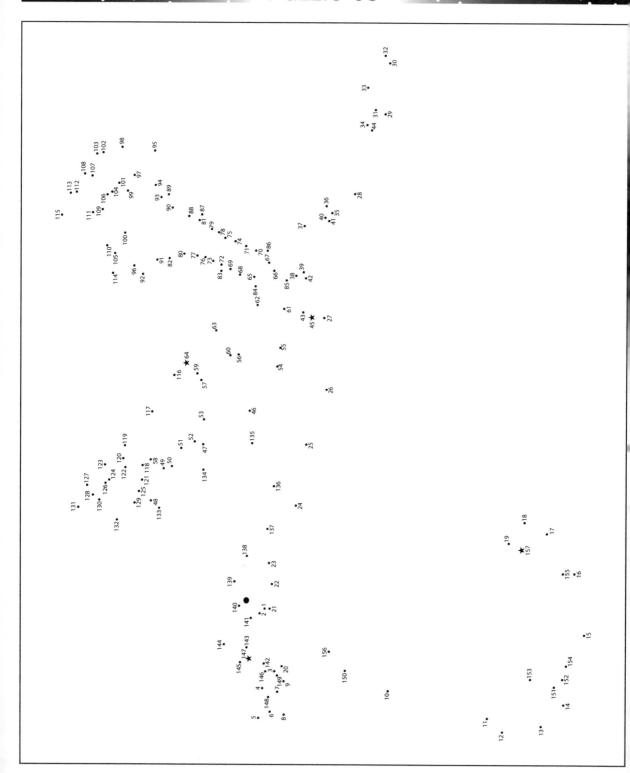

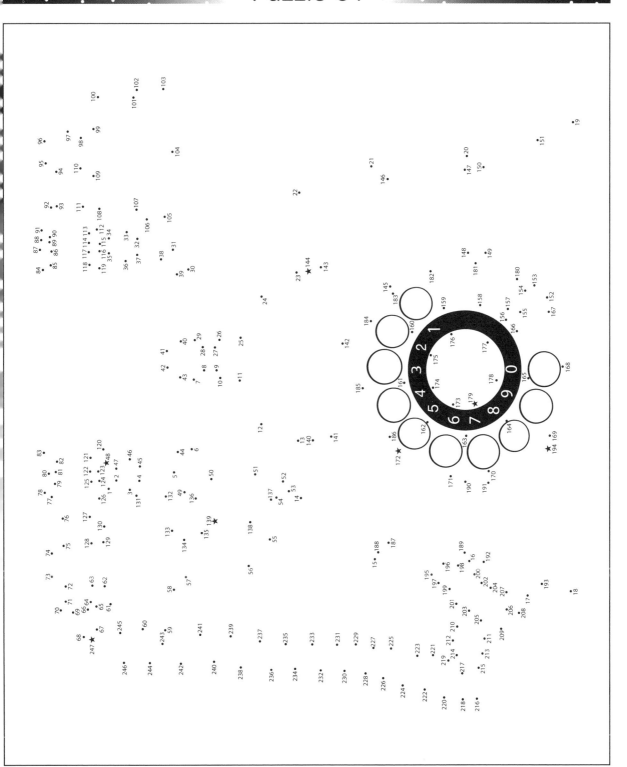

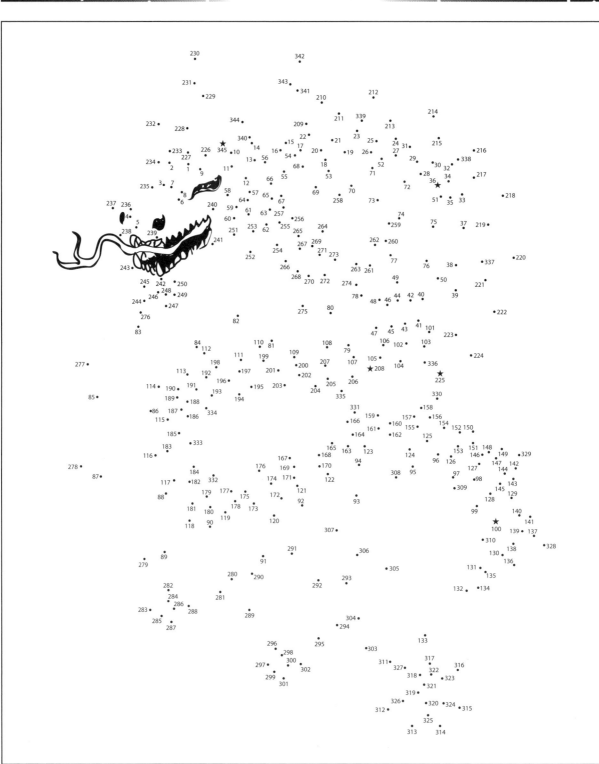

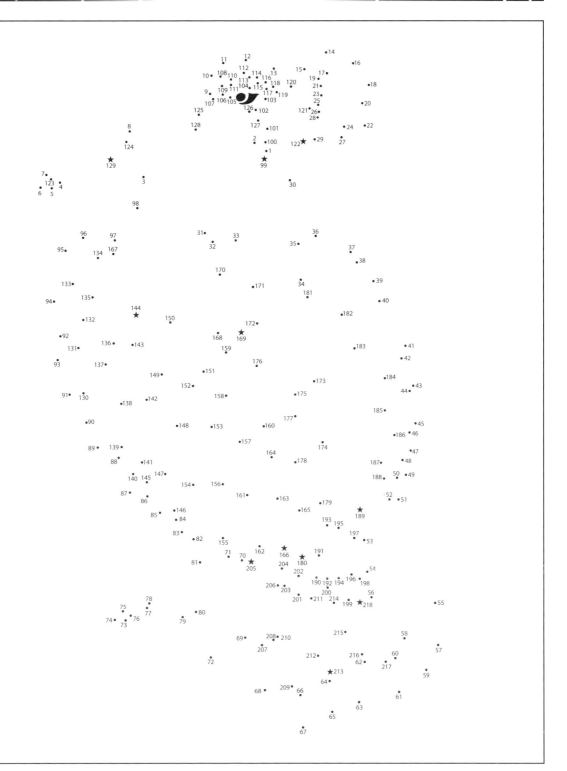

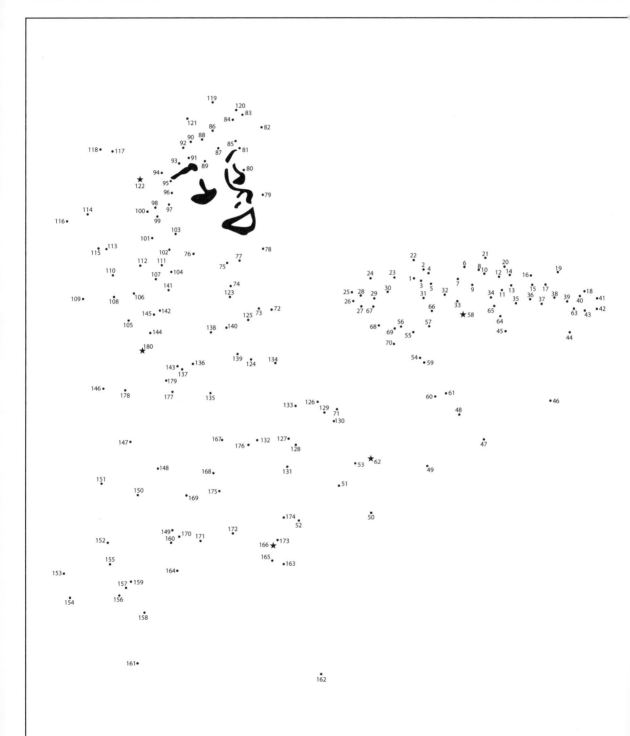

Puzzle 68

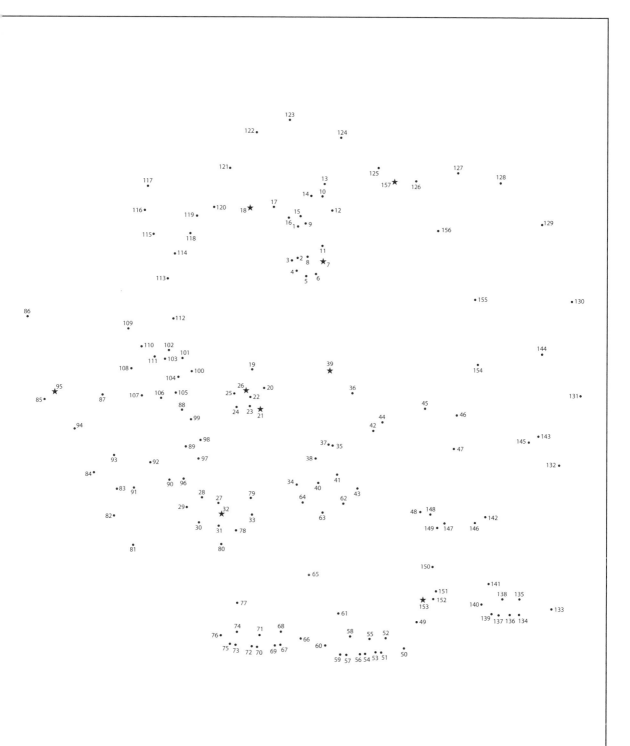

71

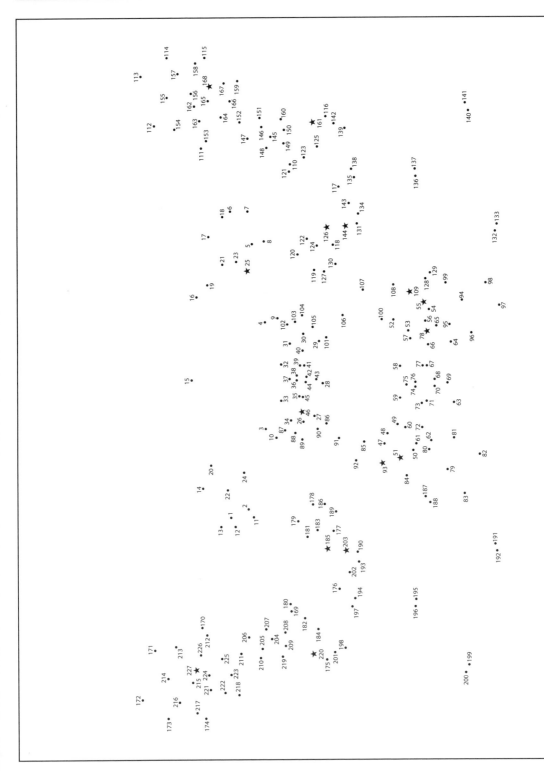

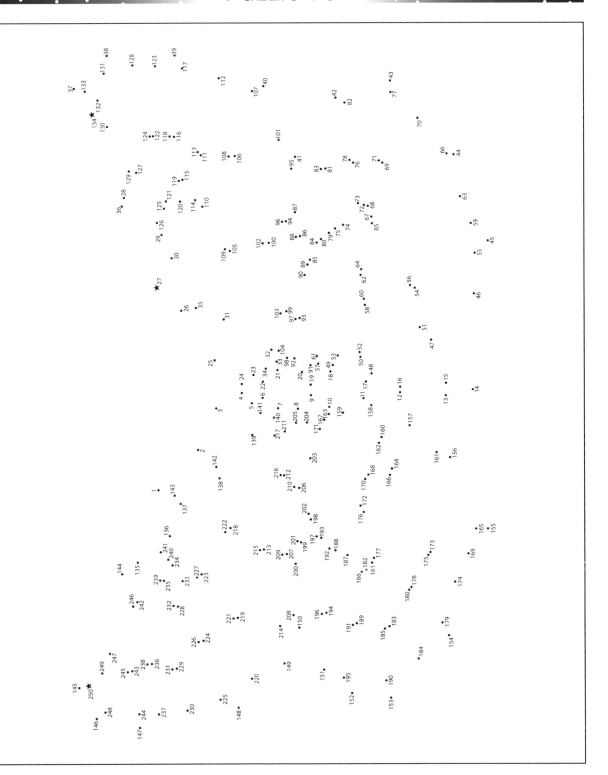

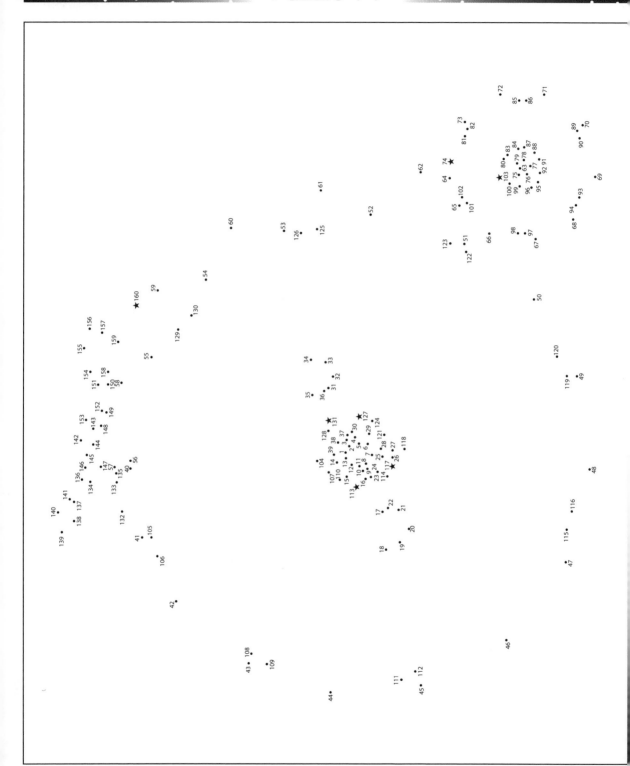

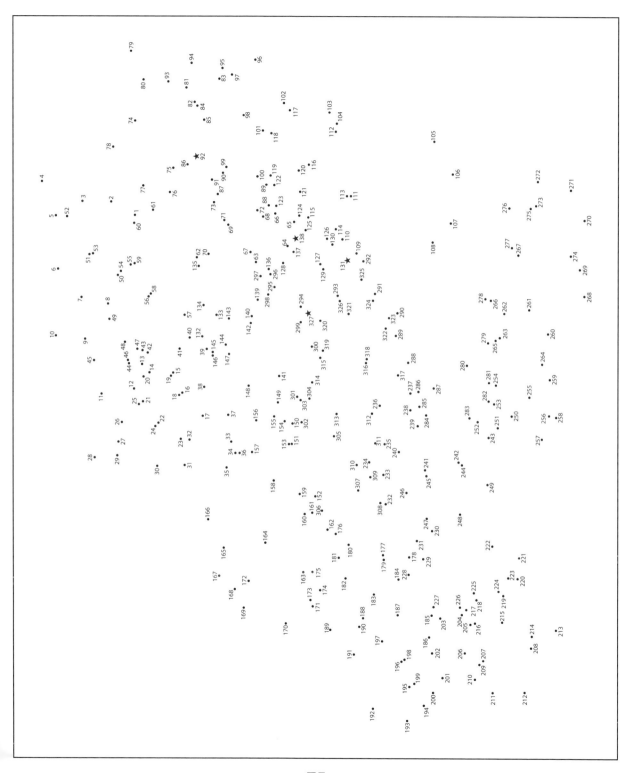

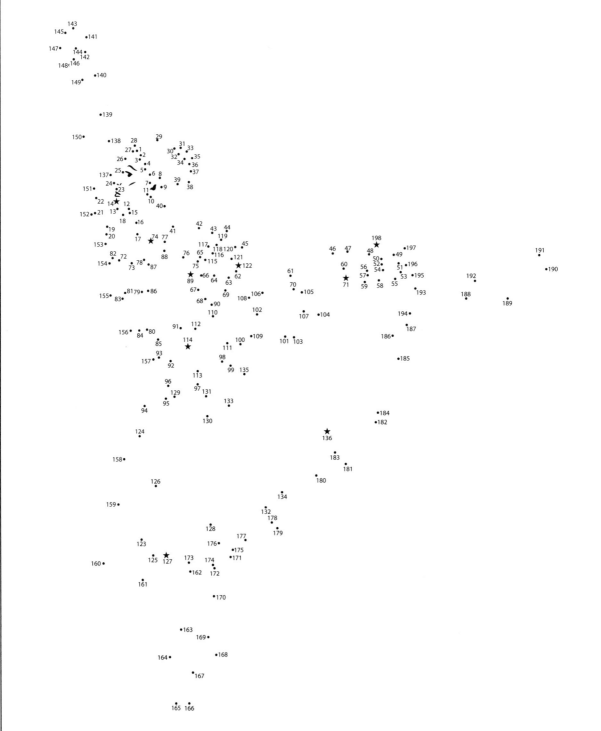

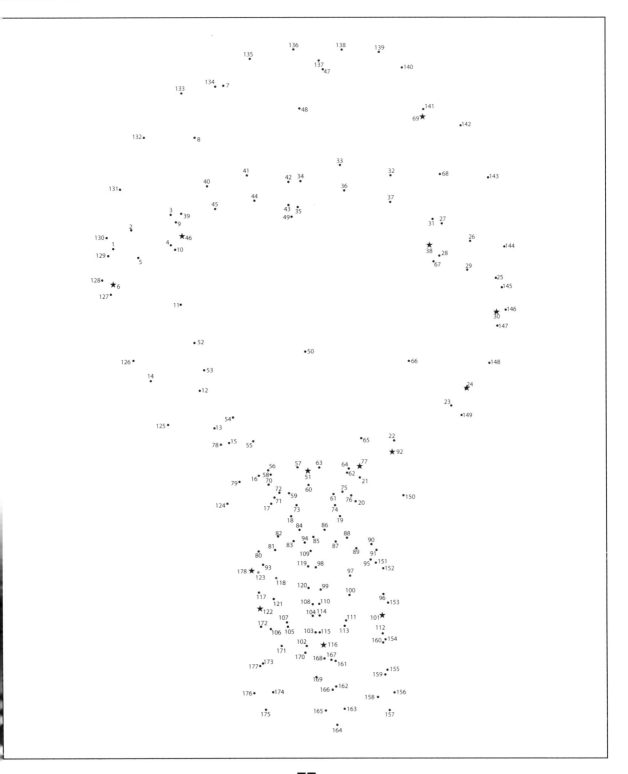

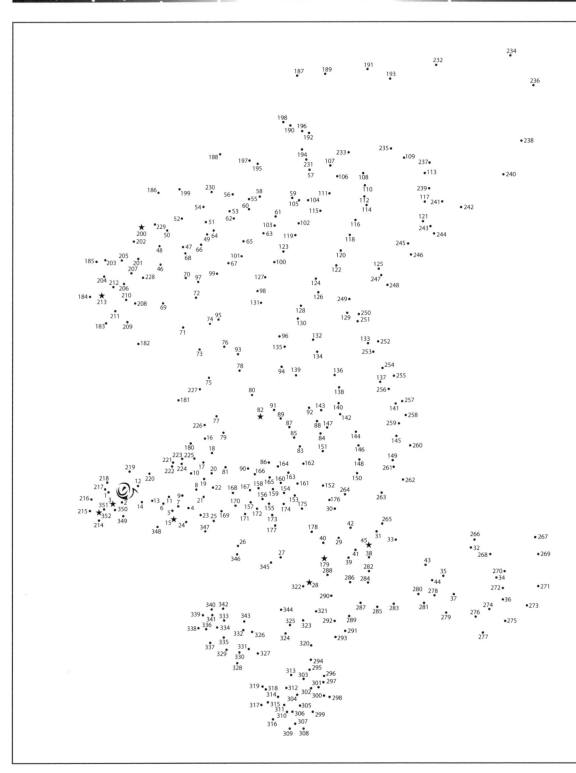

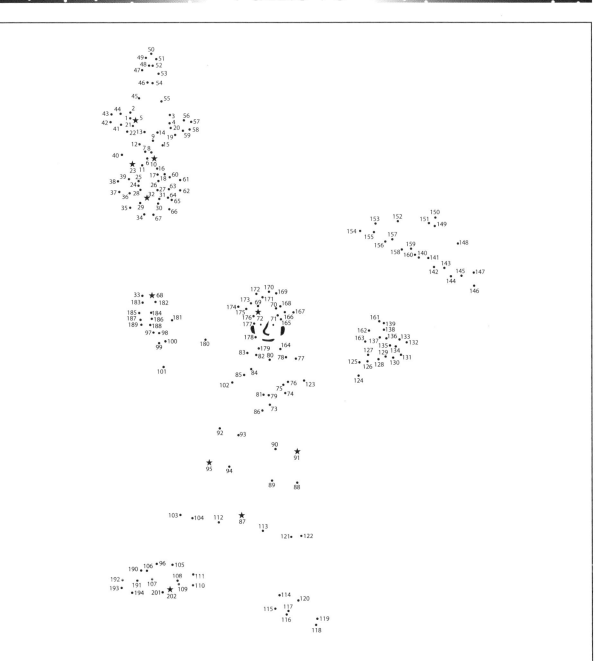

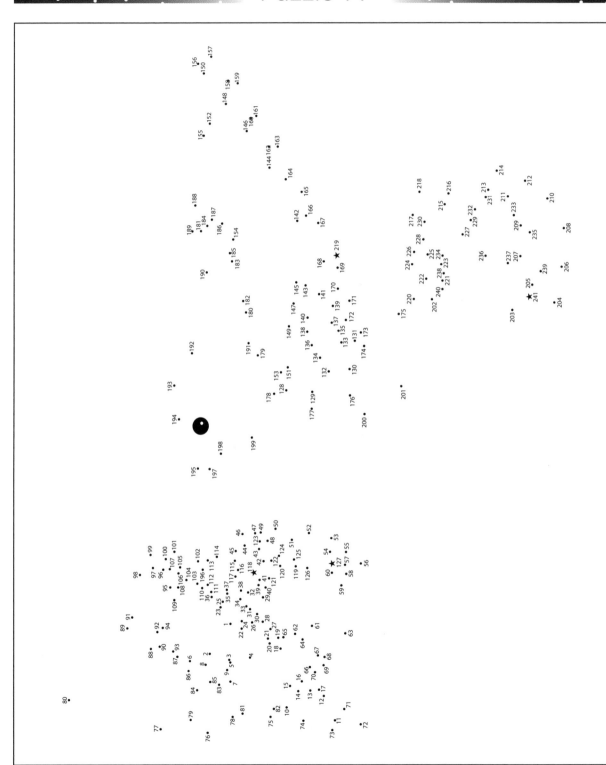

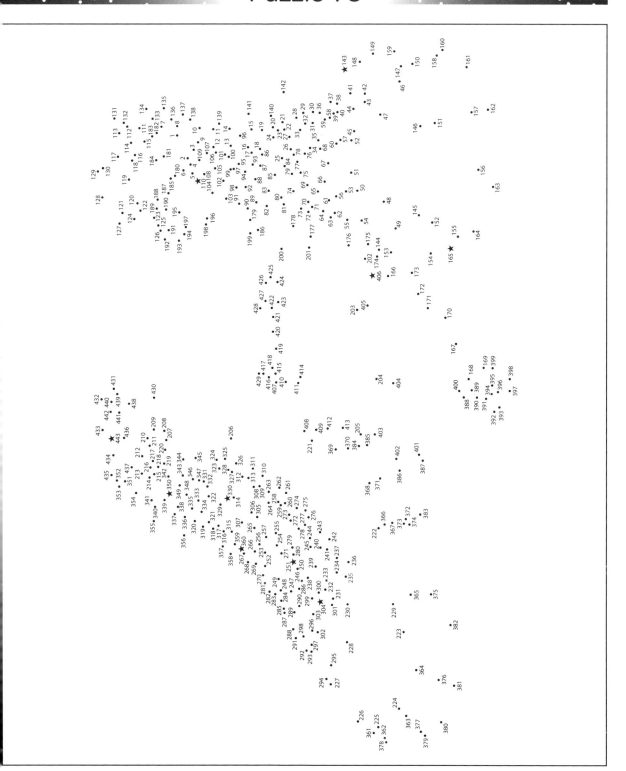

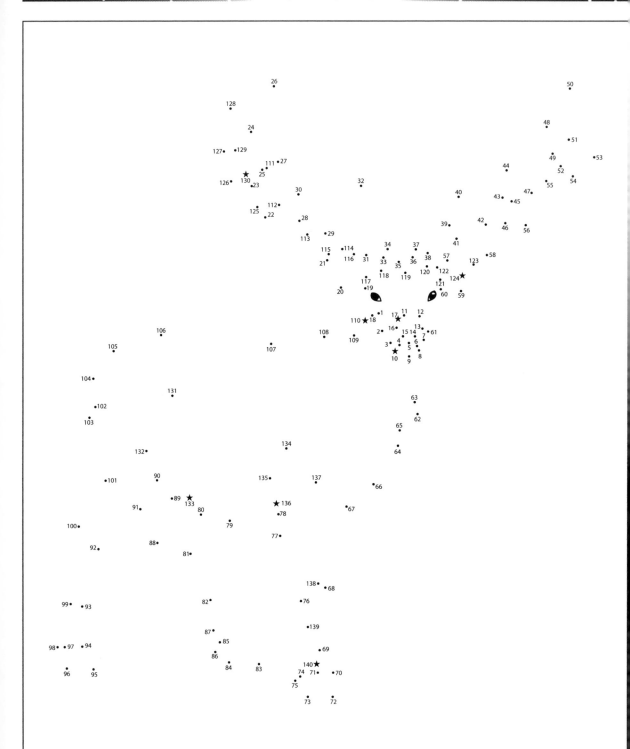

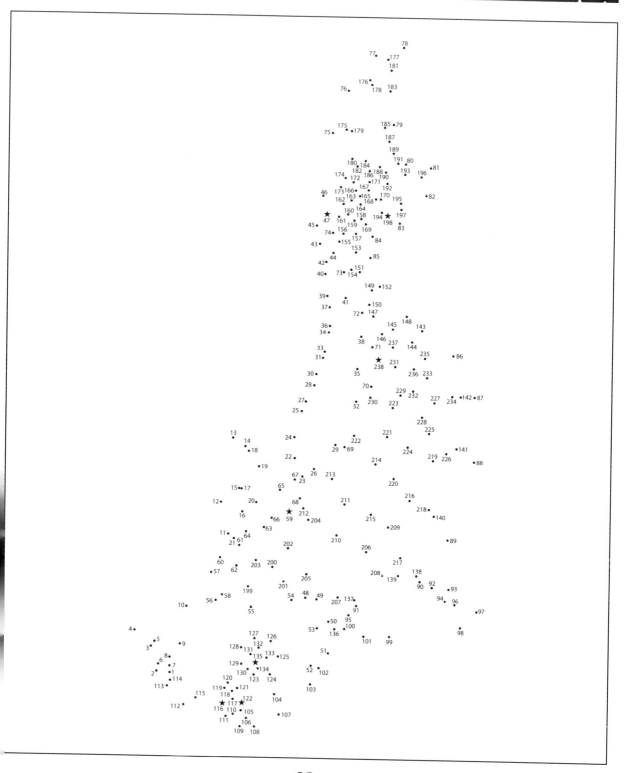

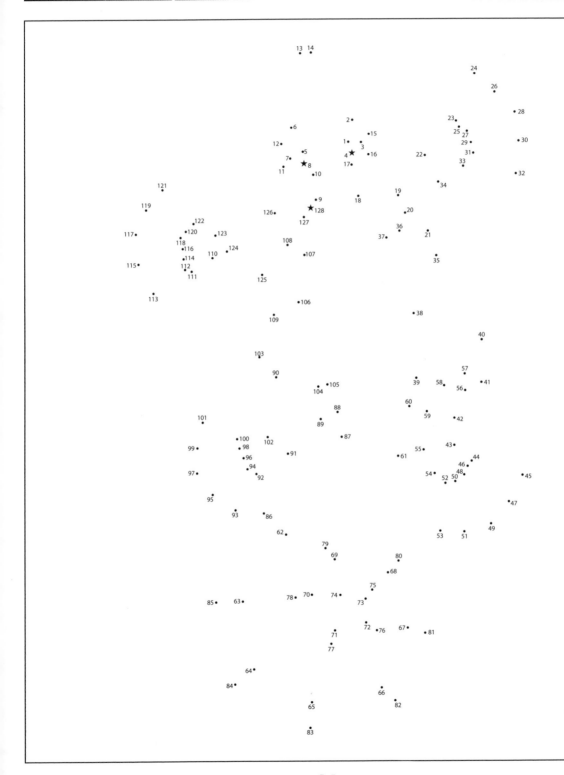

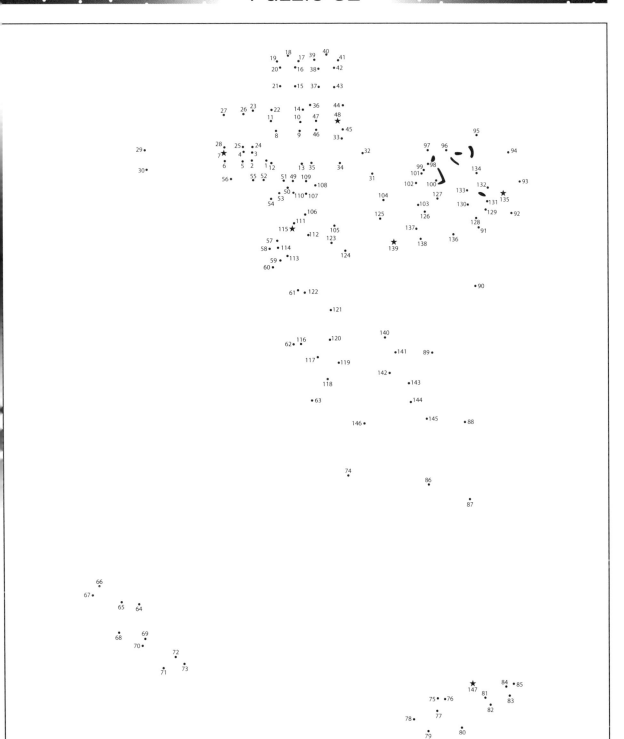

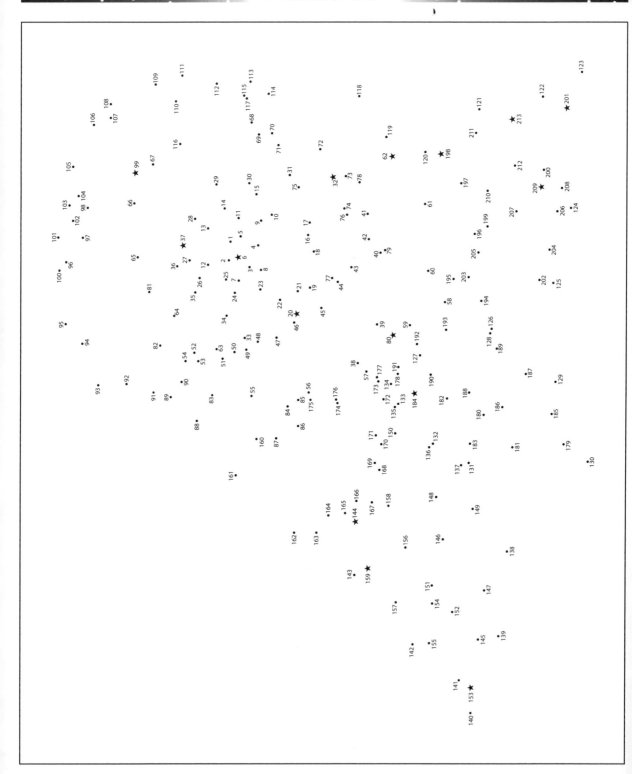

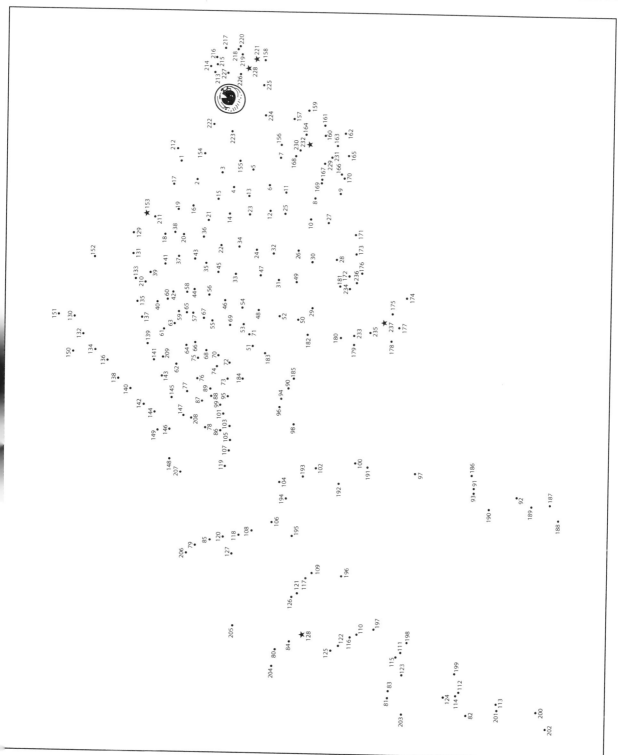

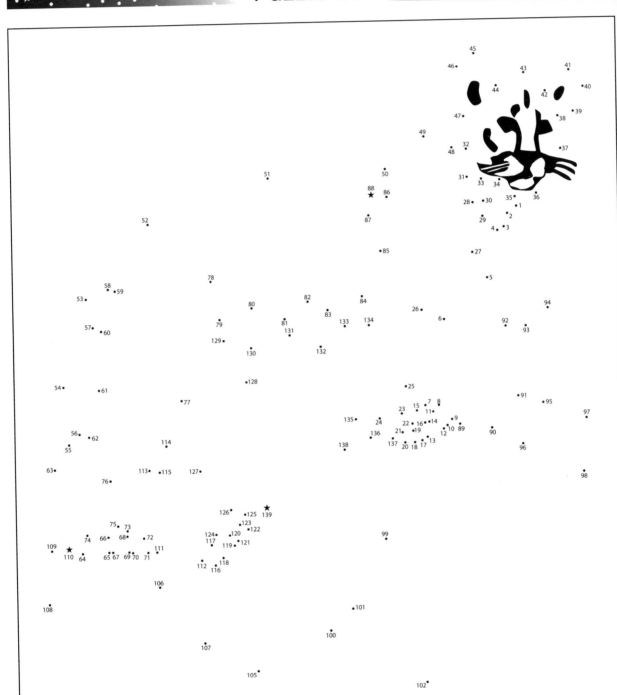

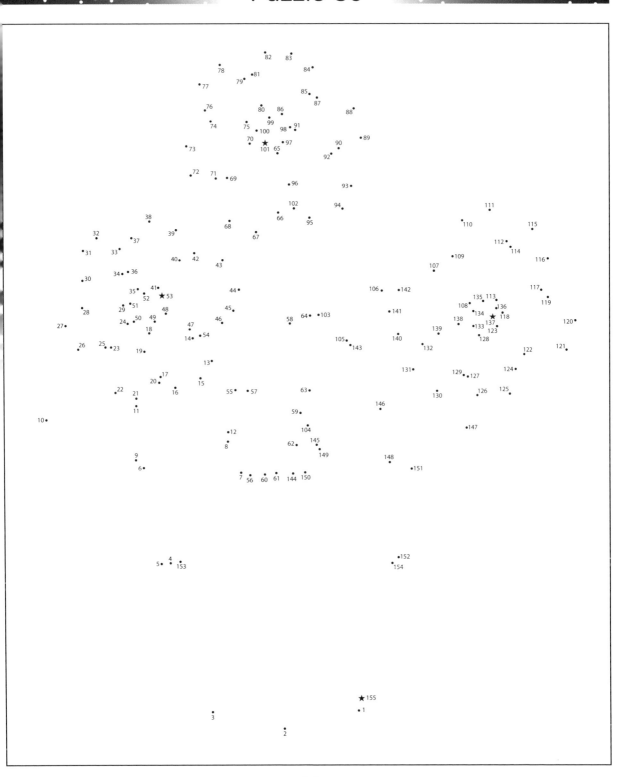

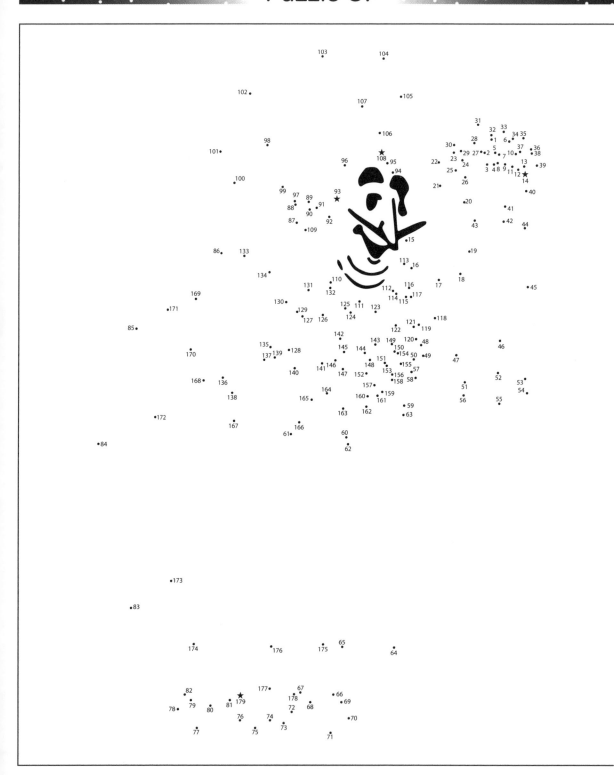

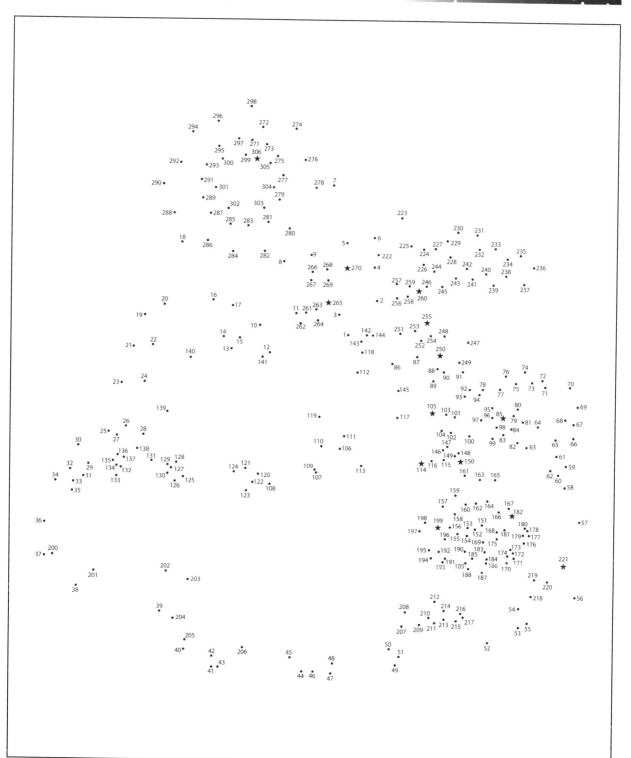

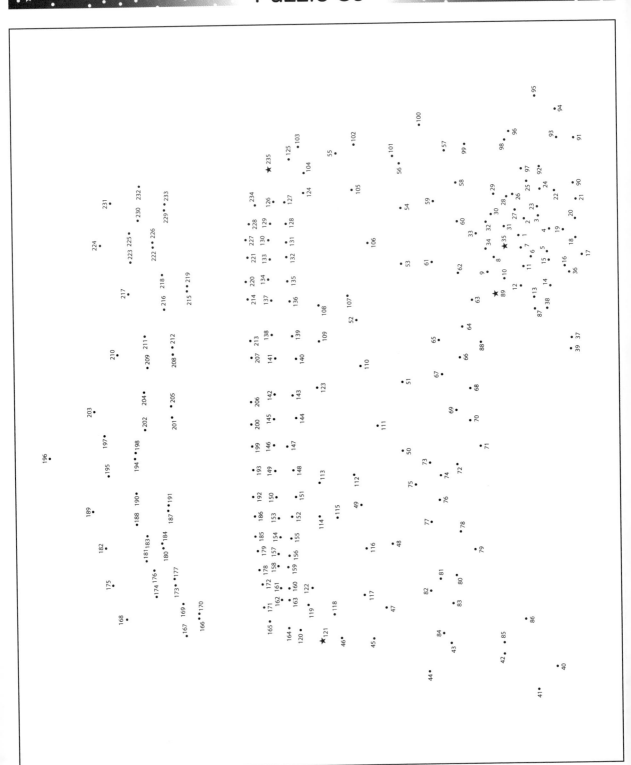

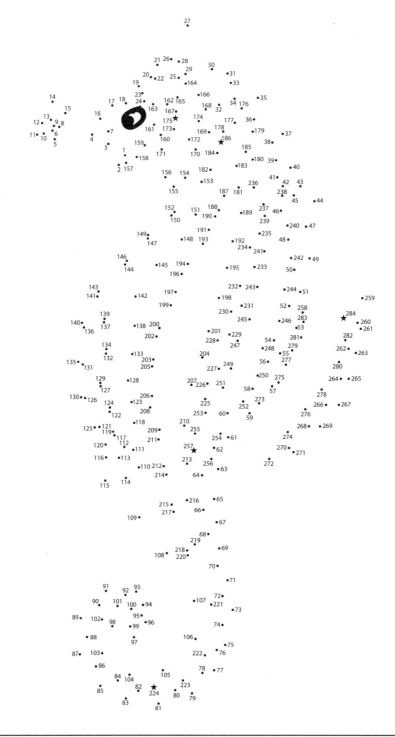

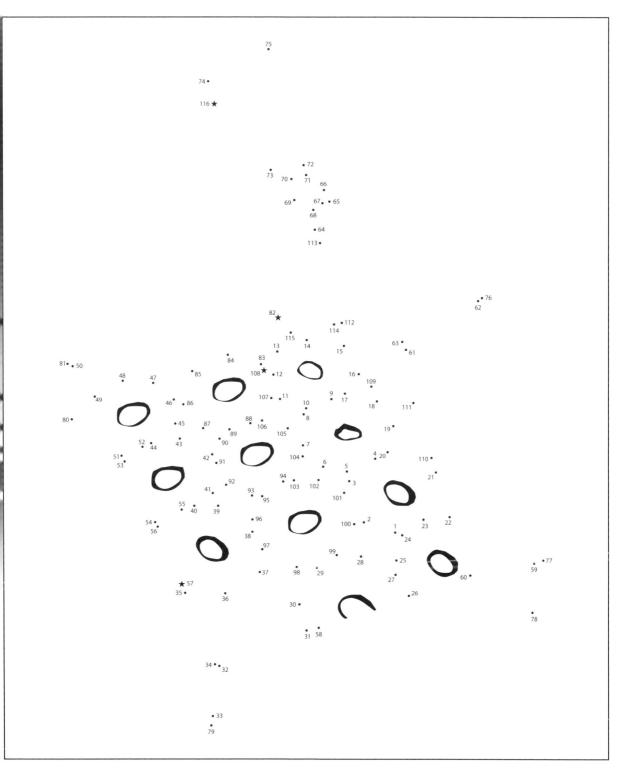

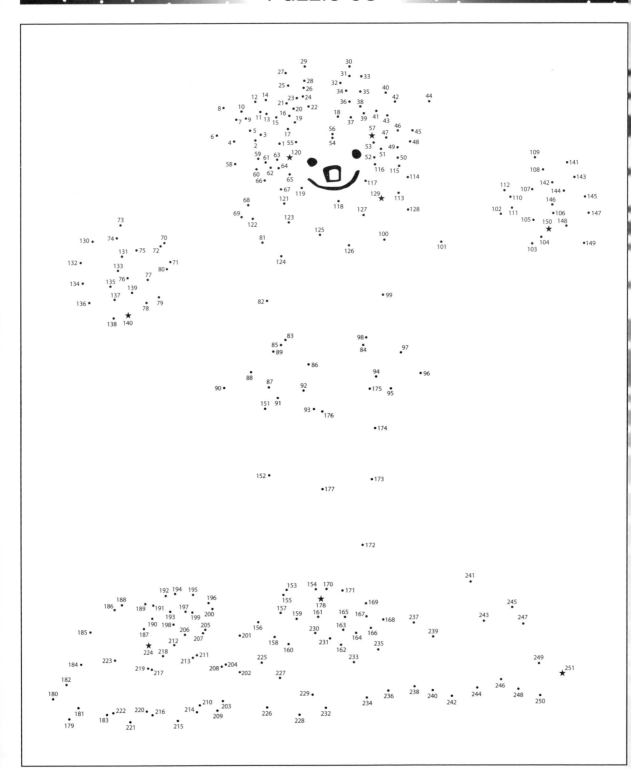

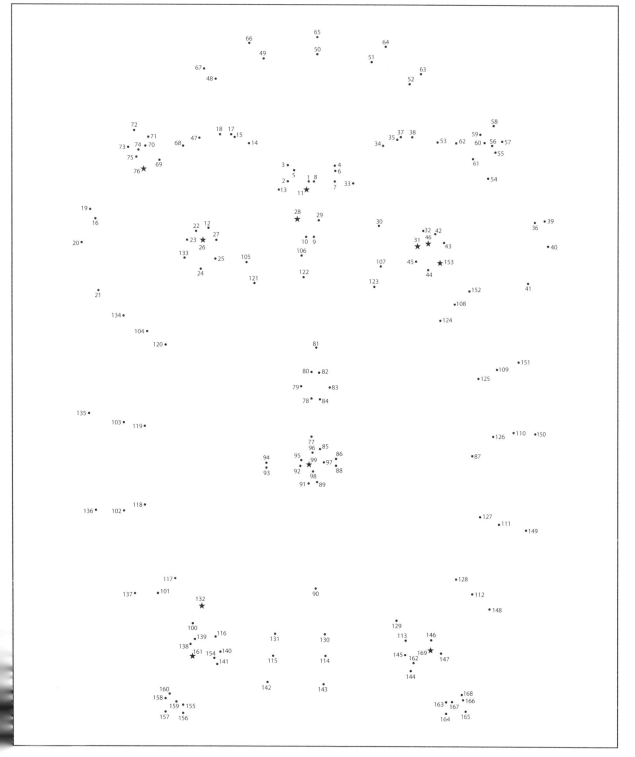

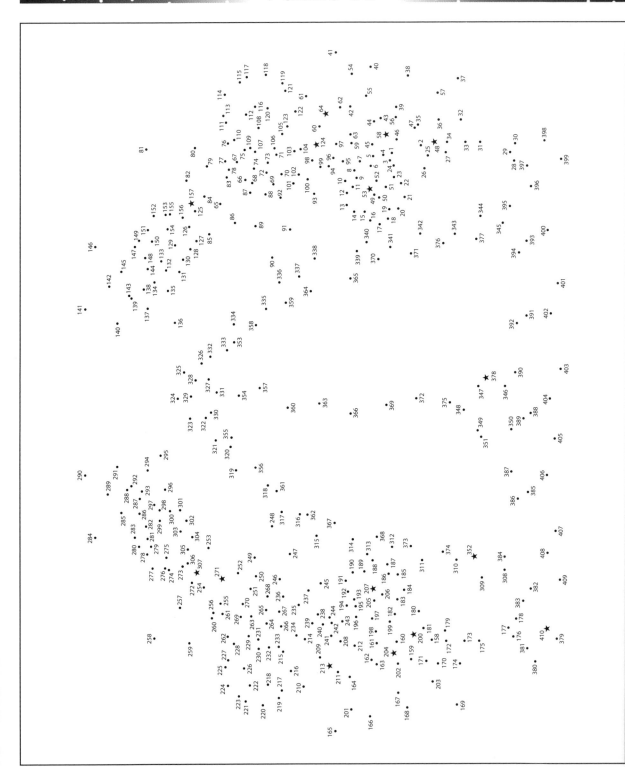

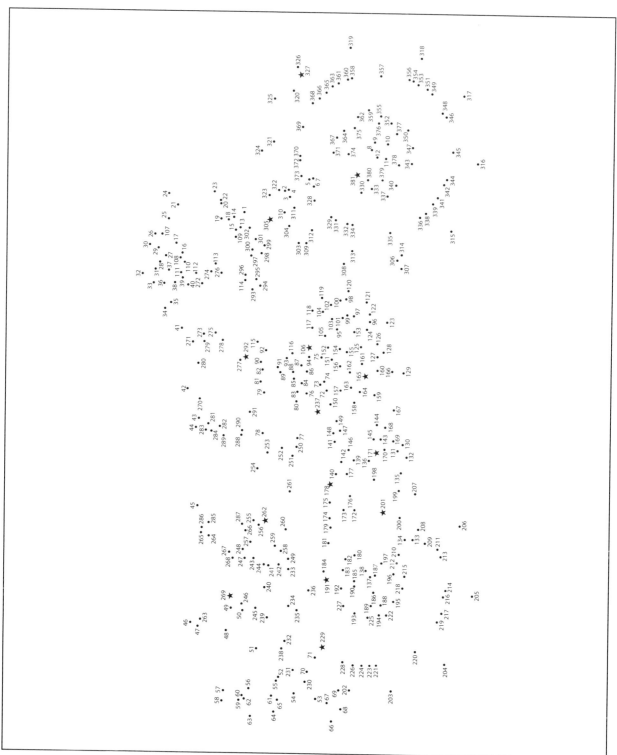

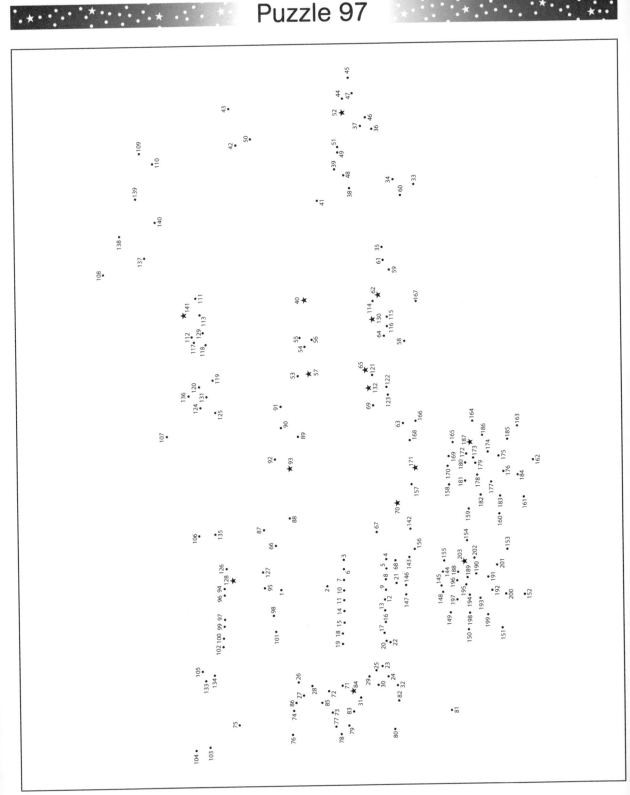

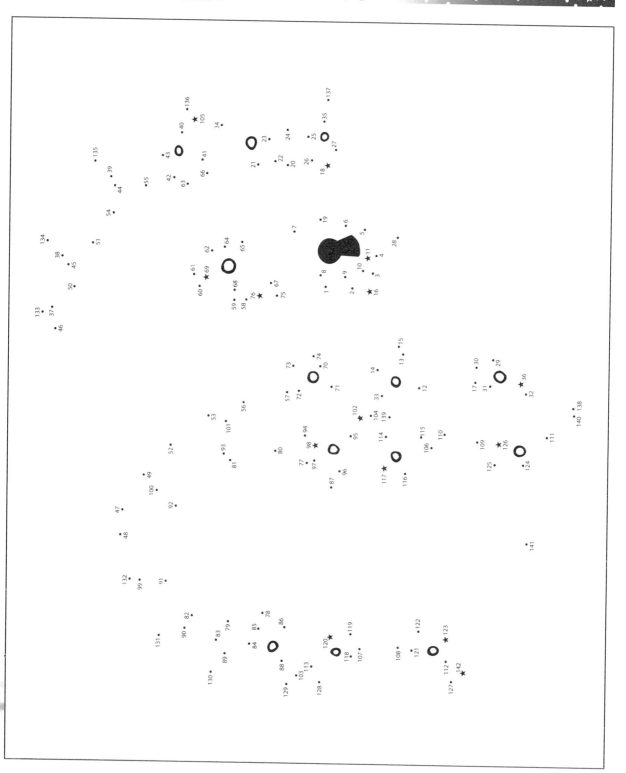

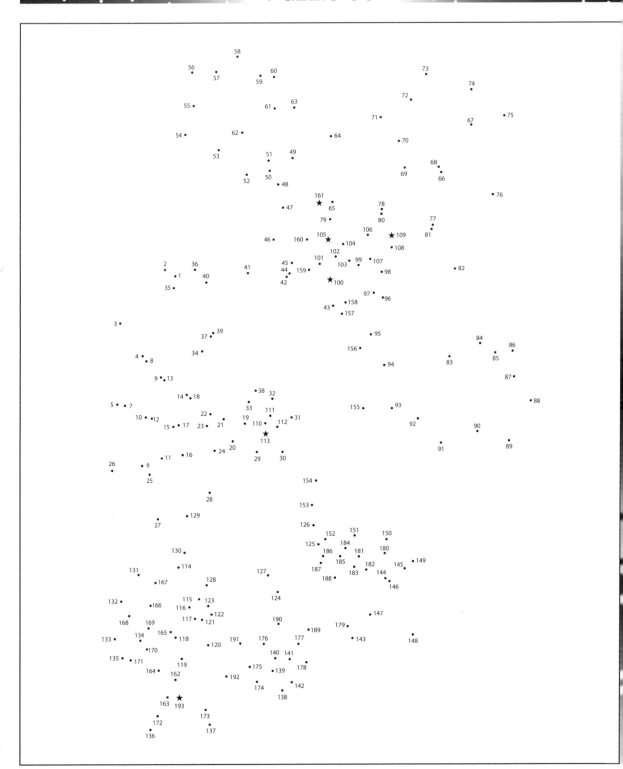

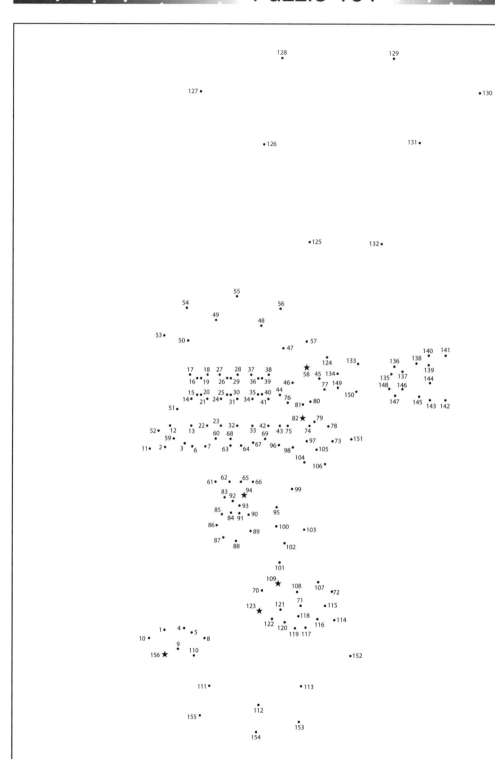

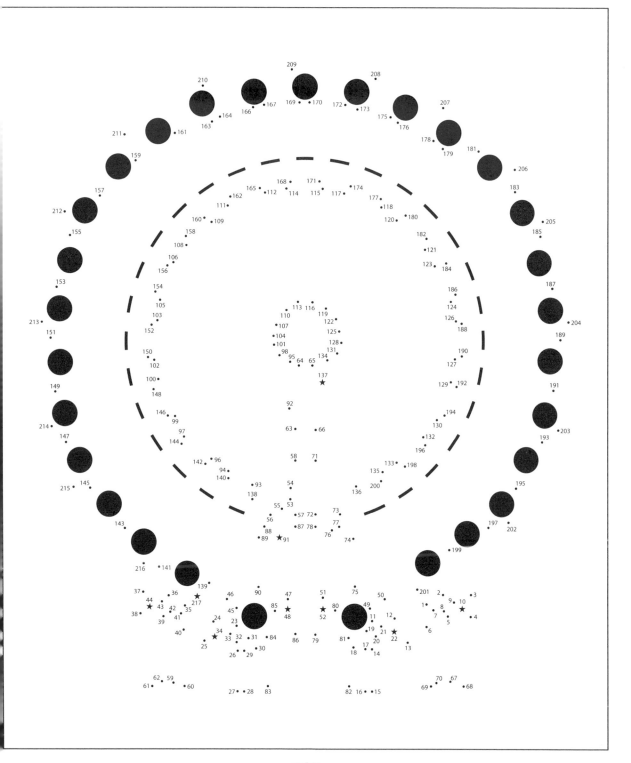

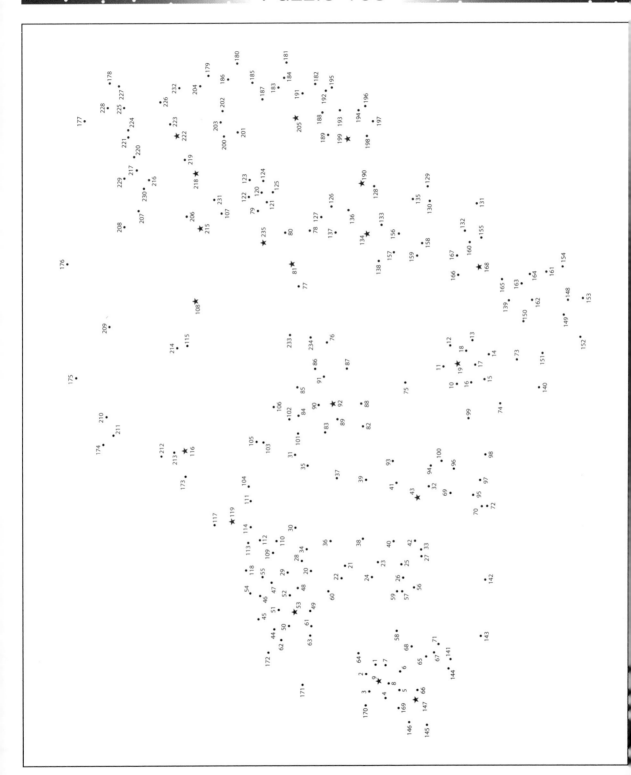

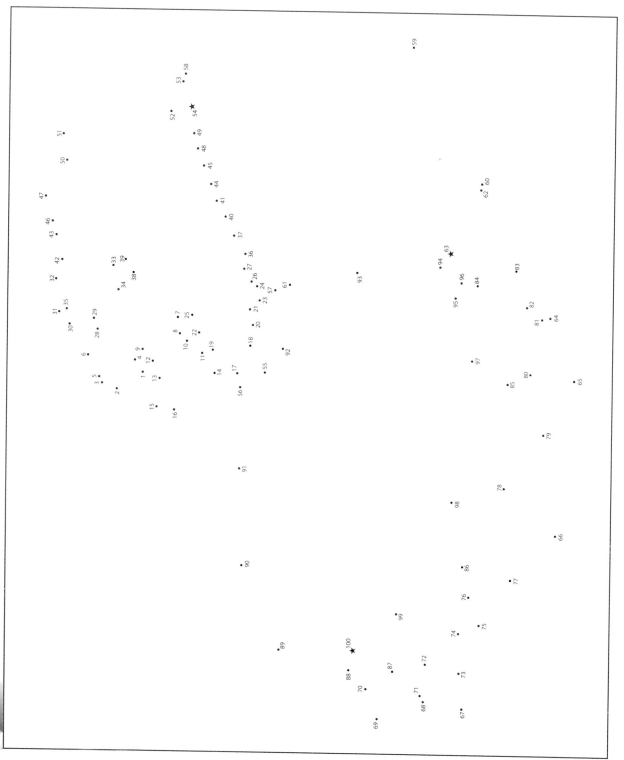

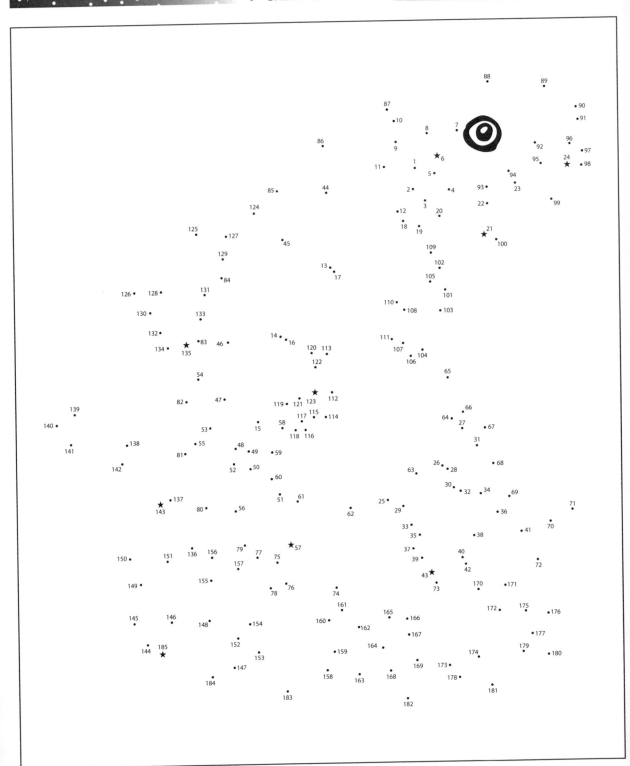

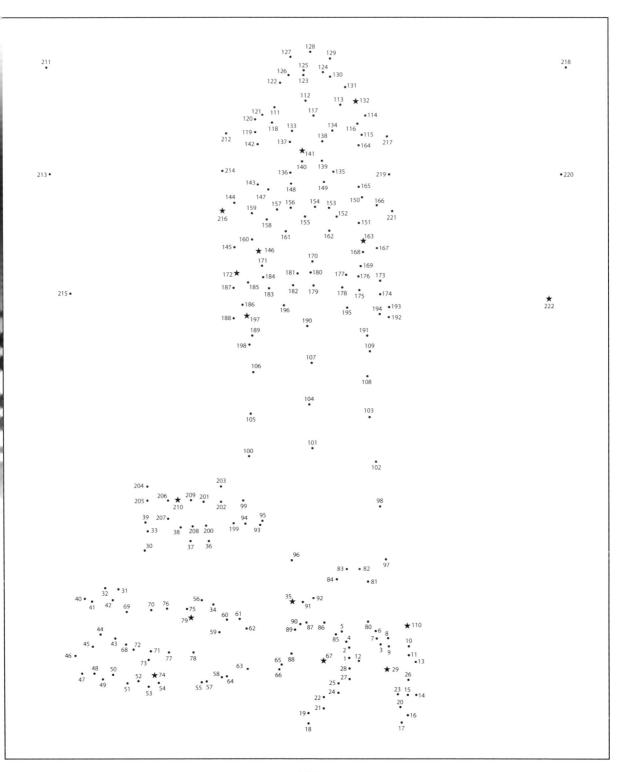

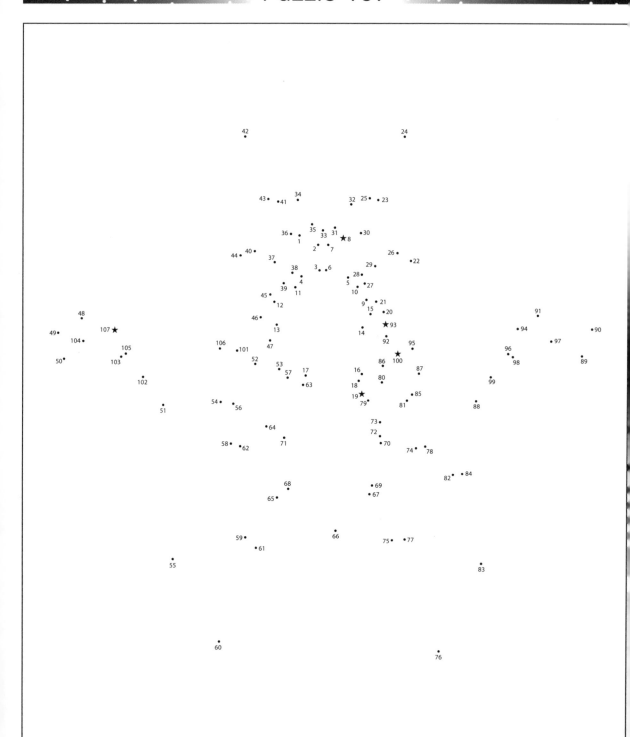

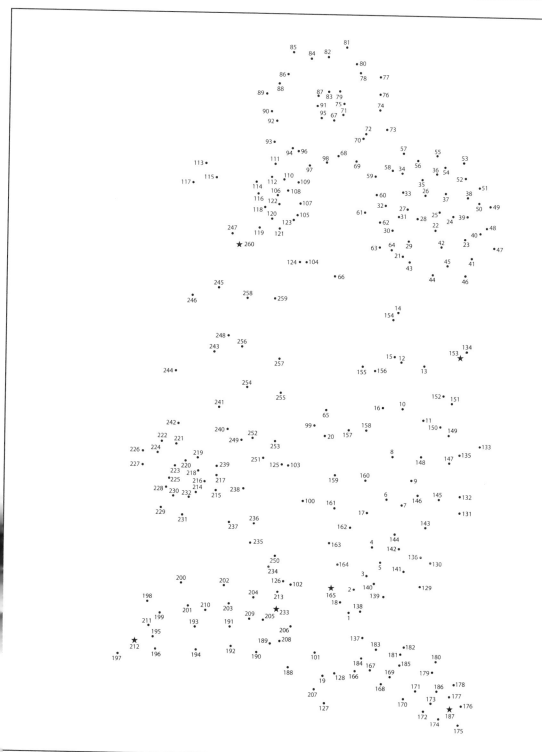

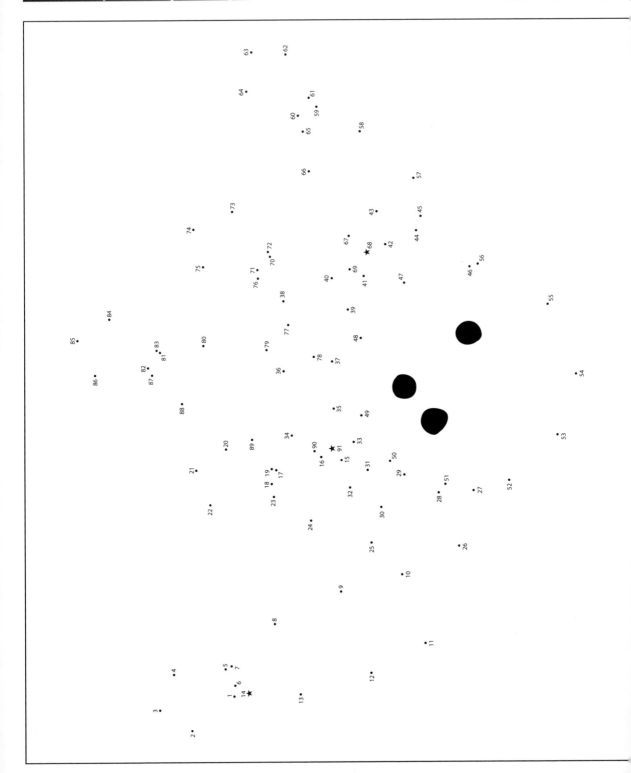

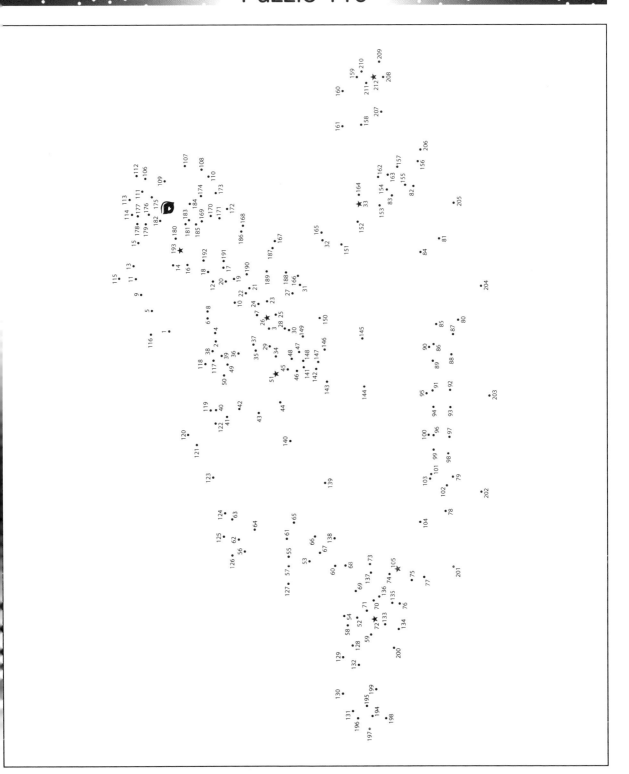

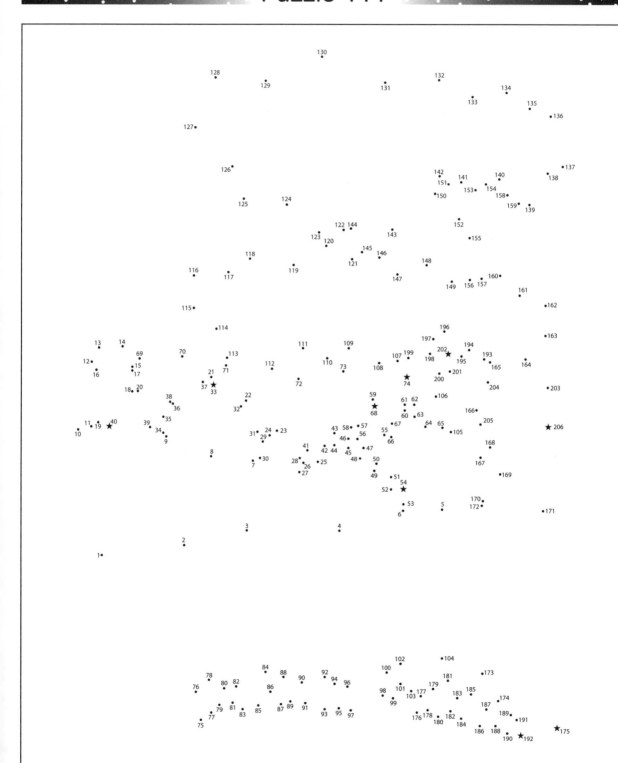

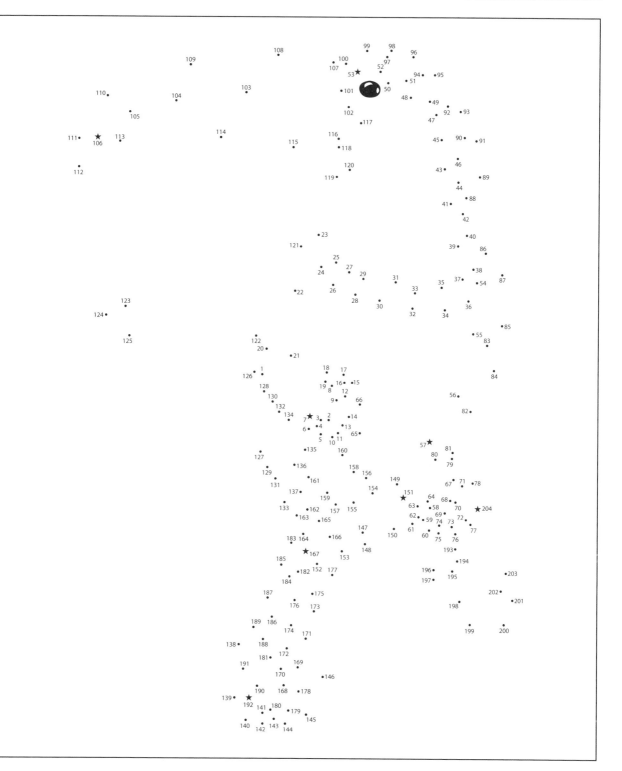

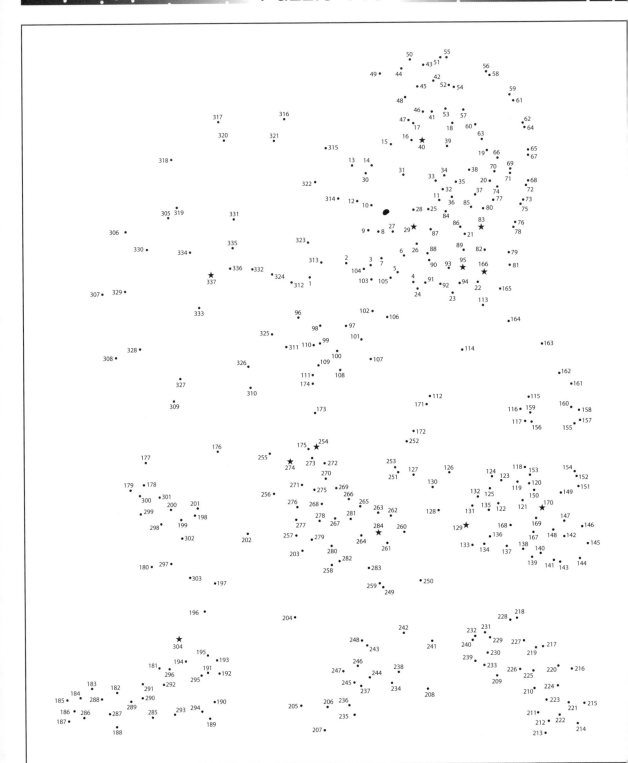

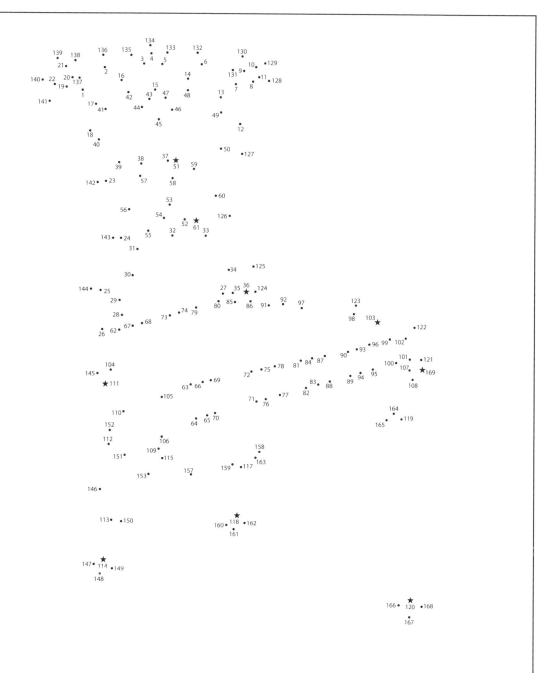

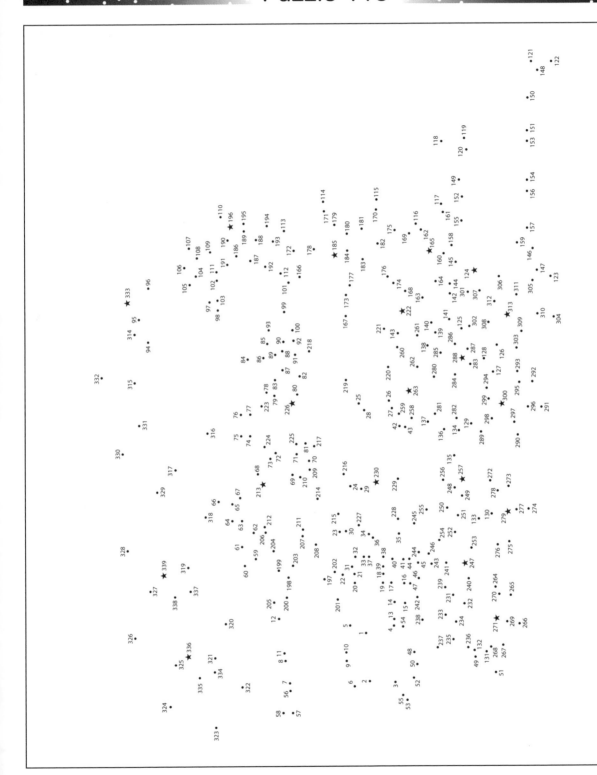

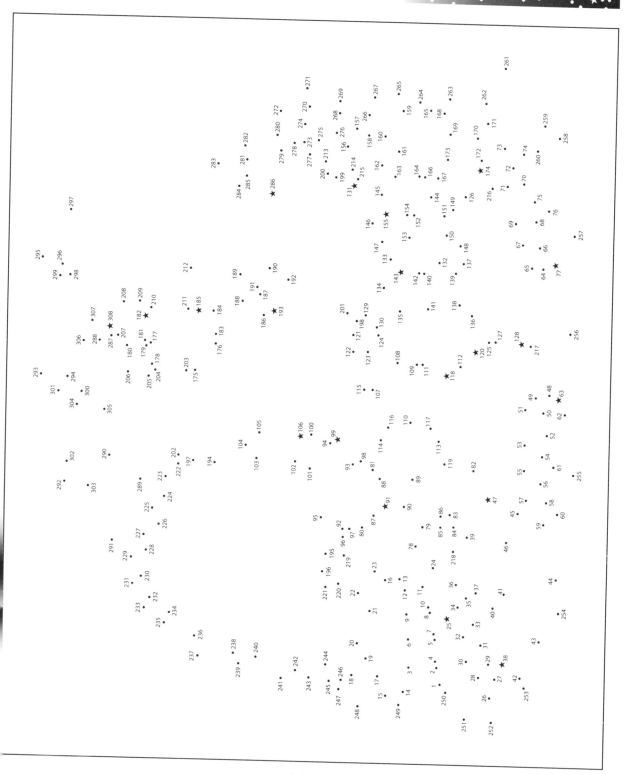

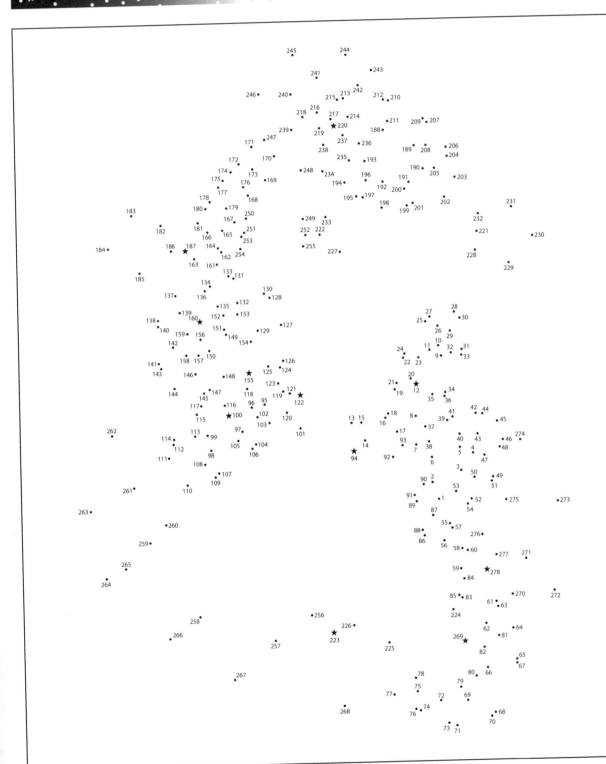

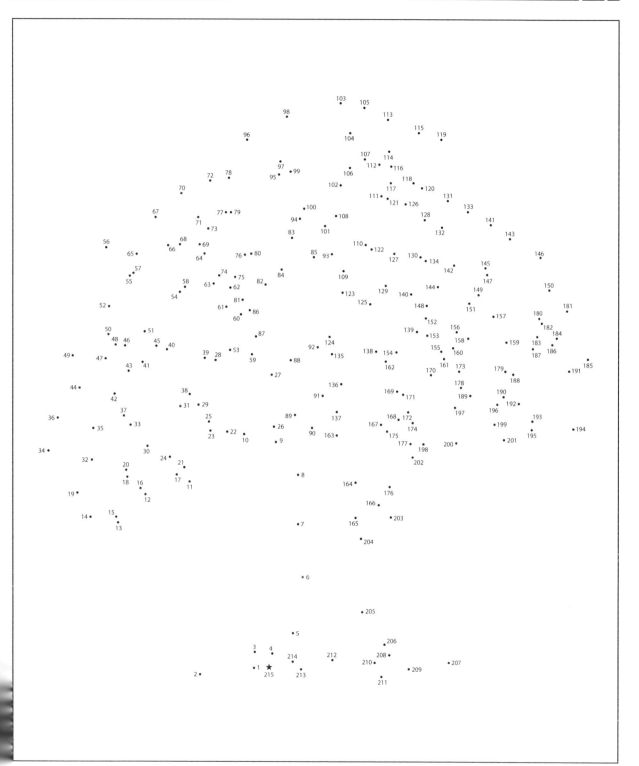

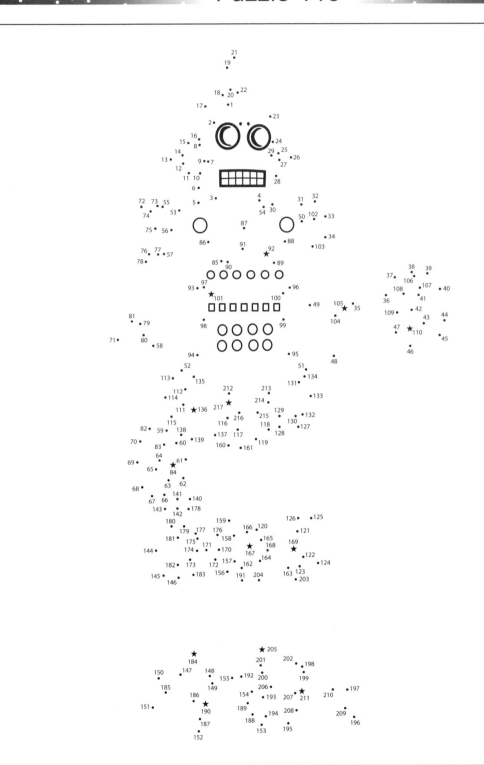

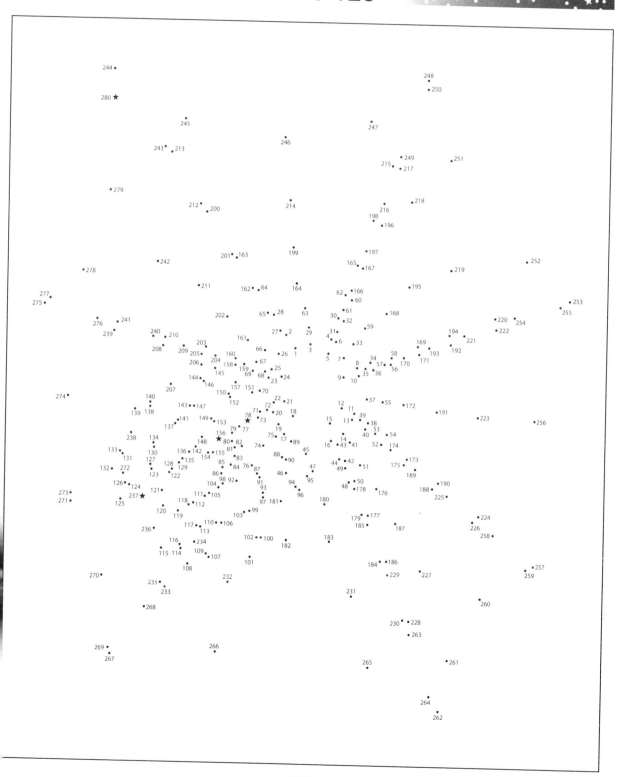

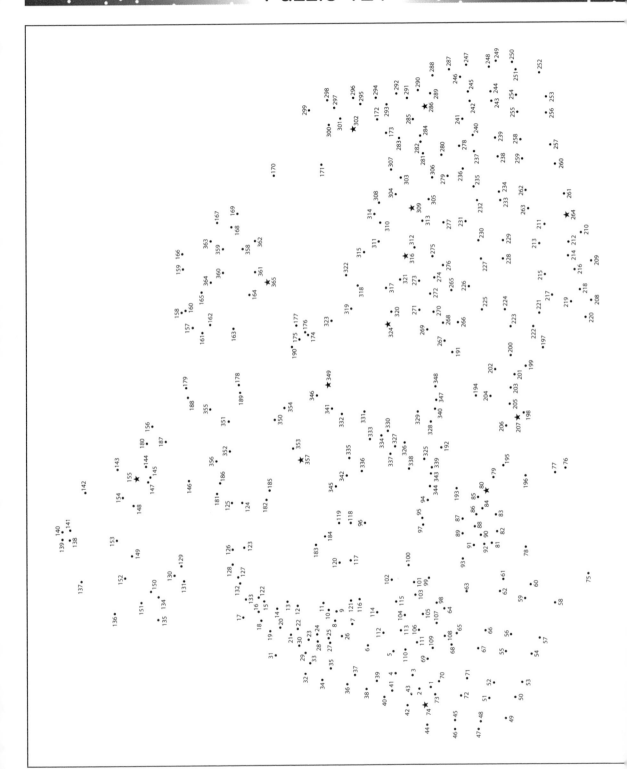

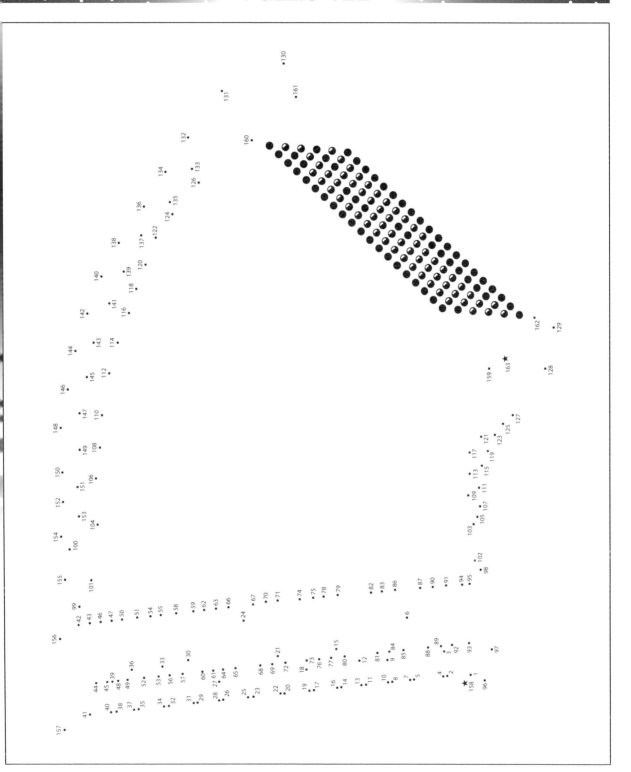

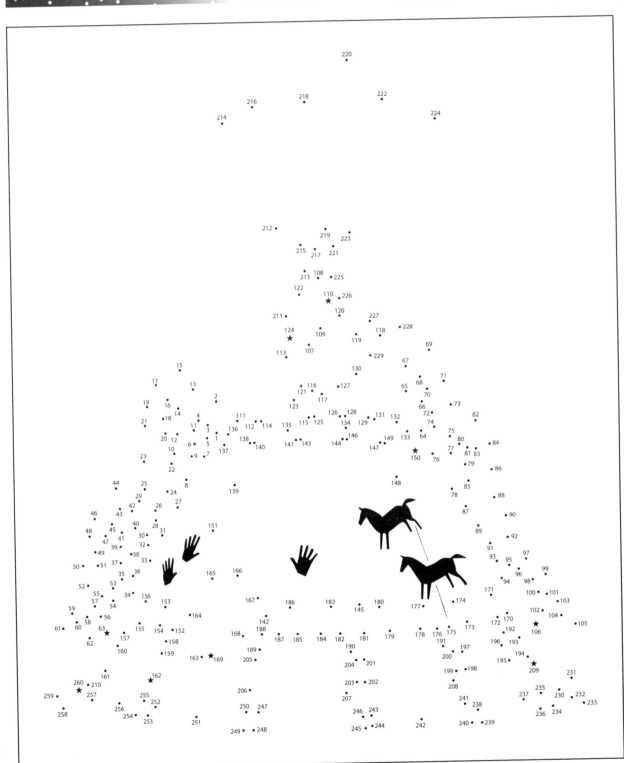

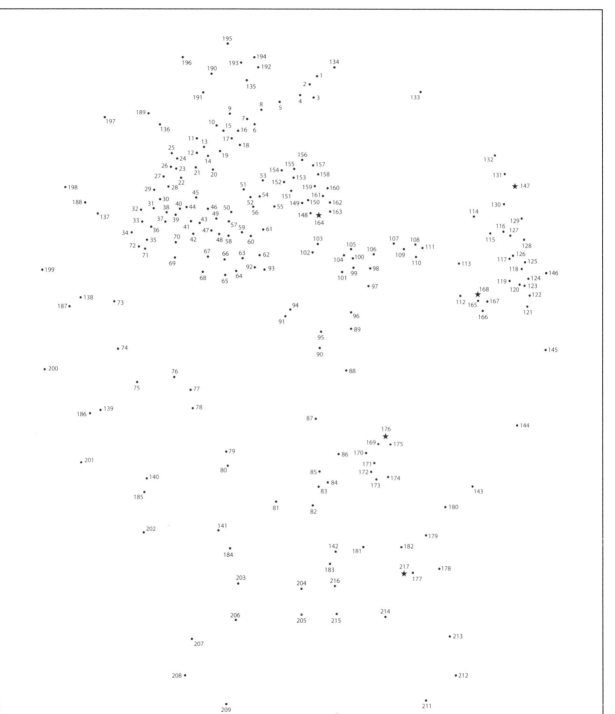

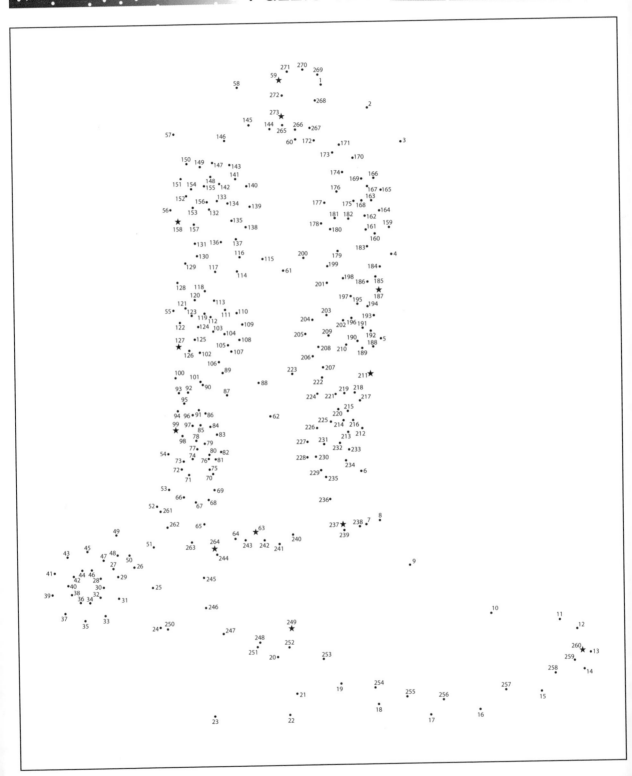

Puzzle 1

Puzzle 2

Puzzle 3

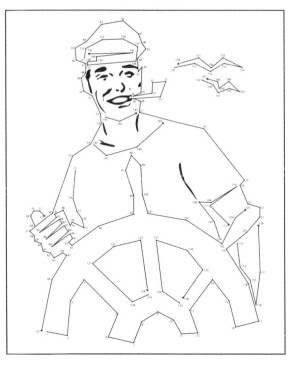

Puzzle 4

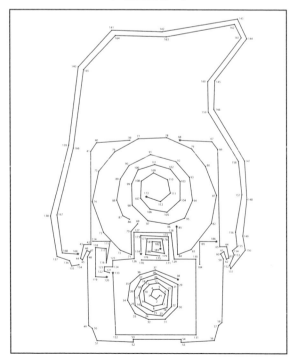

Puzzle 5

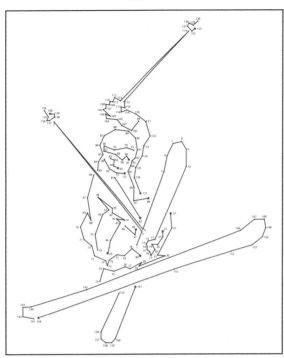

Puzzle 6

Puzzle 7

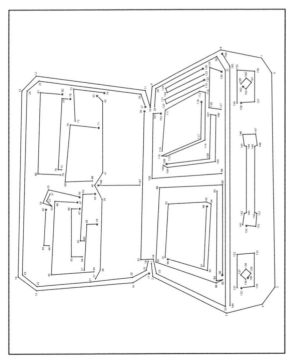

Puzzle 8

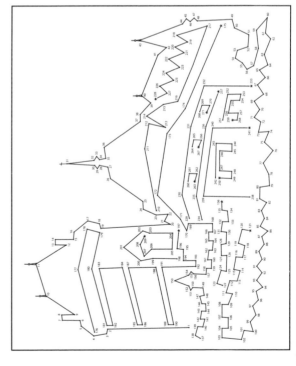

130

Puzzle 9

Puzzle 10

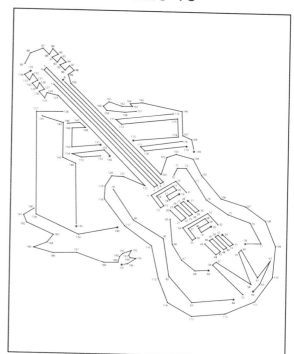

Puzzle 11

Puzzle 12

131

Puzzle 13

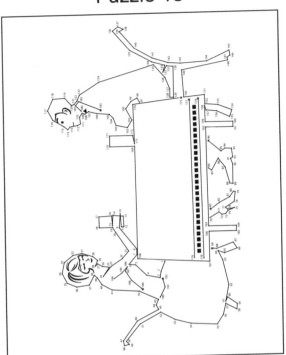

Puzzle 14

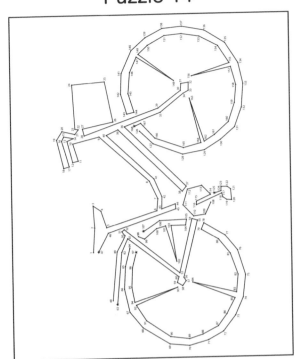

Puzzle 15

Puzzle 16

Puzzle 17

Puzzle 18

Puzzle 19

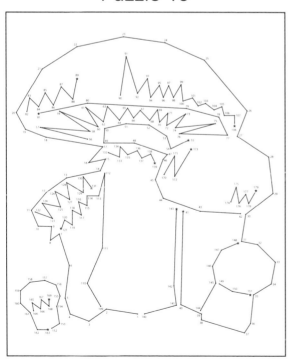

Puzzle 20

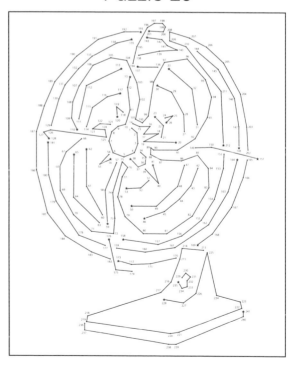

Puzzle 21

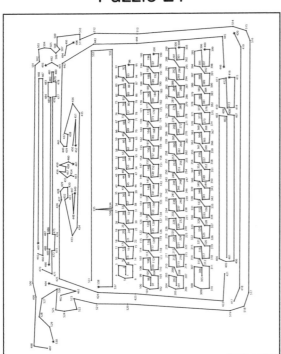

Puzzle 22

Puzzle 23

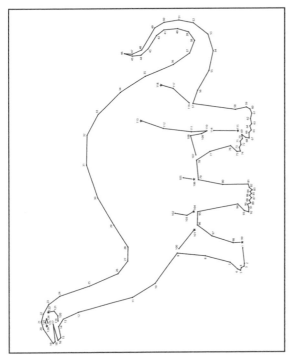

Puzzle 24

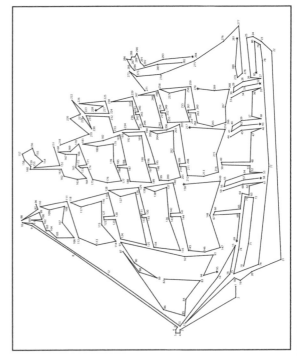

Puzzle 25

Puzzle 26

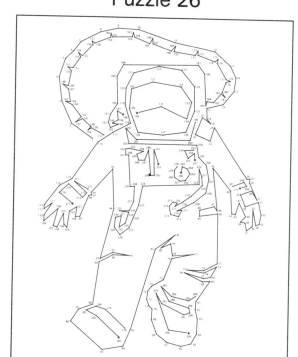

Puzzle 27

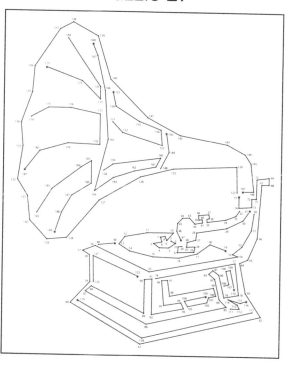

Puzzle 28

135

Puzzle 29

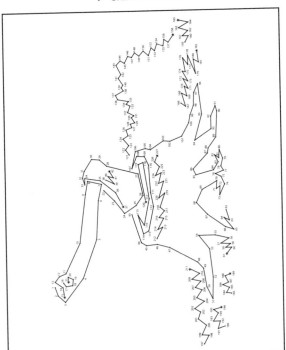

Puzzle 30

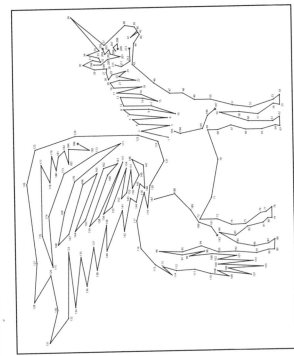

Puzzle 31

Puzzle 32

Puzzle 33

Puzzle 34

Puzzle 35

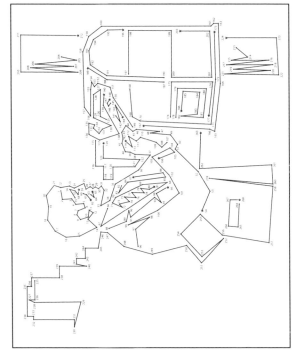

Puzzle 36

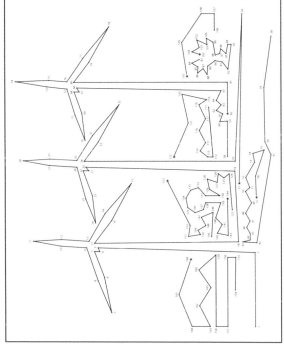

Puzzle 37

Puzzle 38

Puzzle 39

Puzzle 40

Puzzle 41

Puzzle 42

Puzzle 43

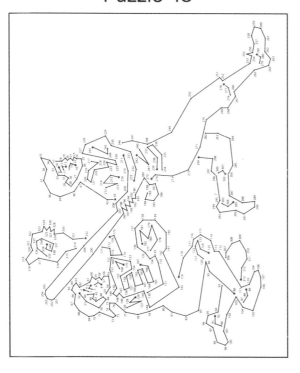

Puzzle 44

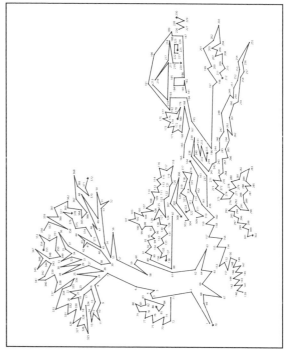

Puzzle 45

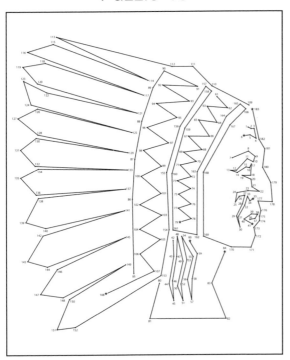

Puzzle 46

Puzzle 47

Puzzle 48

Puzzle 49

Puzzle 50

Puzzle 51

Puzzle 52

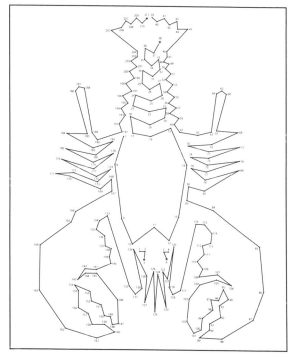

Puzzle 53

Puzzle 54

Puzzle 55

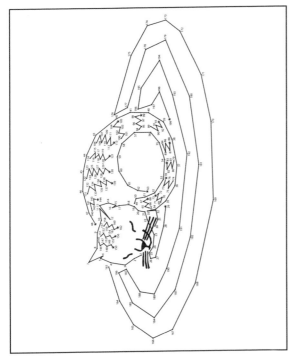

Puzzle 56

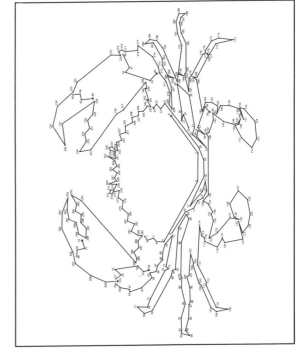

Puzzle 57

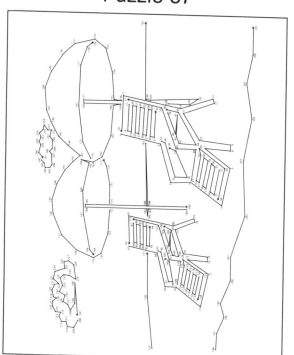

Puzzle 58

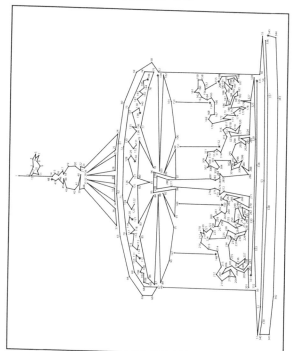

Puzzle 59

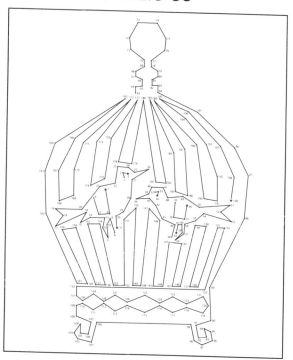

Puzzle 60

Puzzle 61

Puzzle 62

Puzzle 63

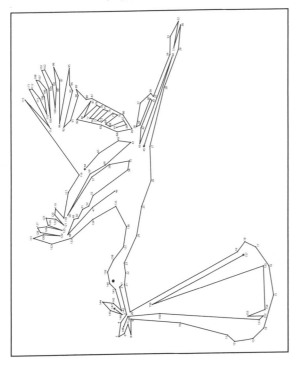

Puzzle 64

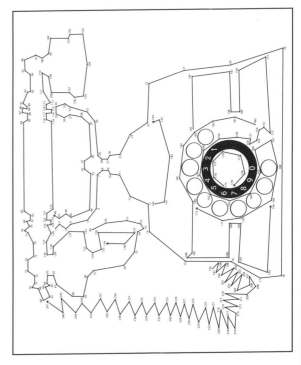

Puzzle 65

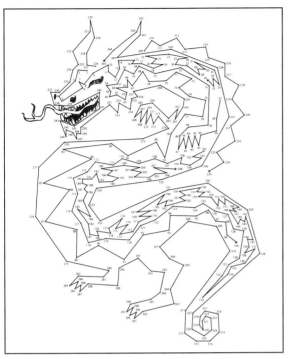

Puzzle 66

Puzzle 67

Puzzle 68

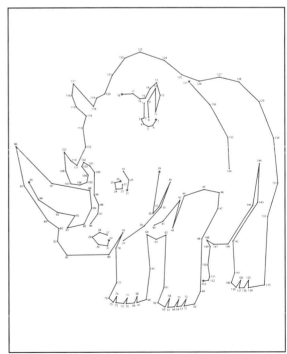

145

Puzzle 69

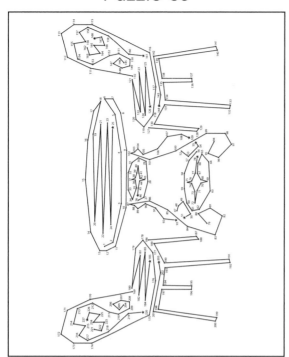

Puzzle 70

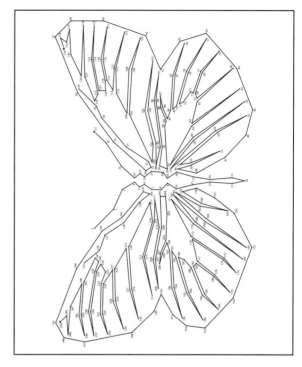

Puzzle 71

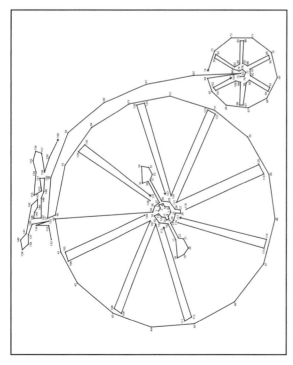

Puzzle 72

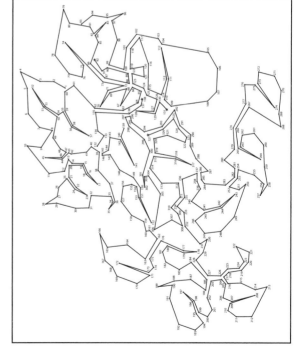

Puzzle 73

Puzzle 74

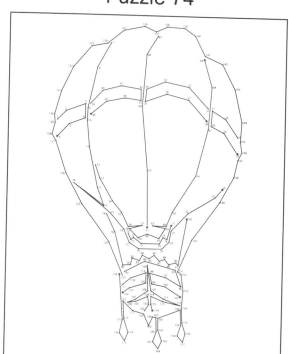

Puzzle 75

Puzzle 76

147

Puzzle 77

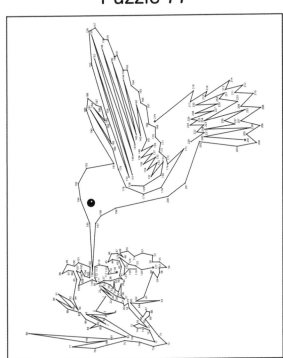

Puzzle 78

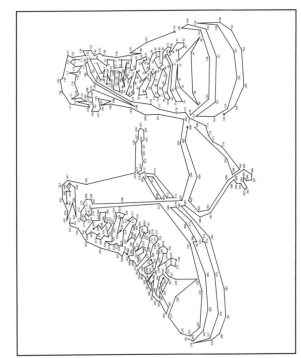

Puzzle 79

Puzzle 80

Puzzle 81

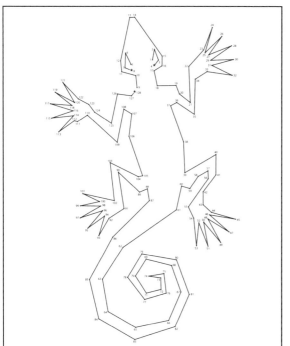

Puzzle 82

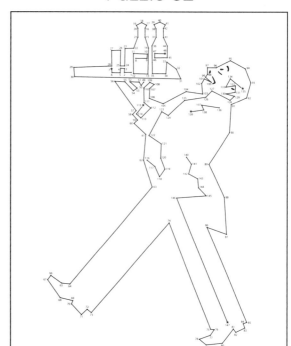

Puzzle 83

Puzzle 84

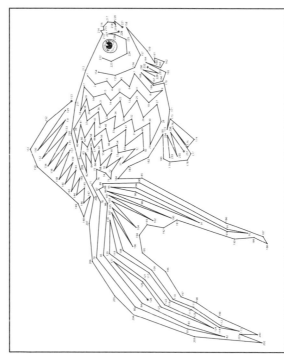

Puzzle 85

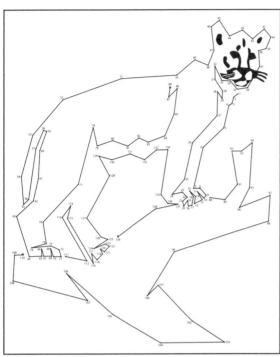

Puzzle 86

Puzzle 87

Puzzle 88

150

Puzzle 89

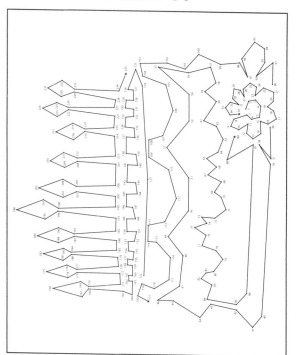

Puzzle 90

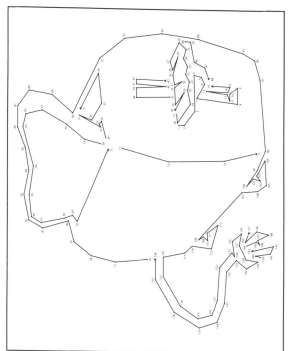

Puzzle 91

Puzzle 92

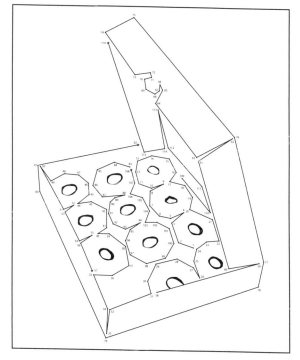

Puzzle 93

Puzzle 94

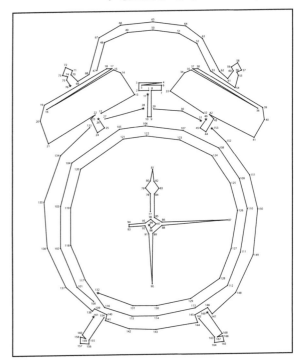

Puzzle 95

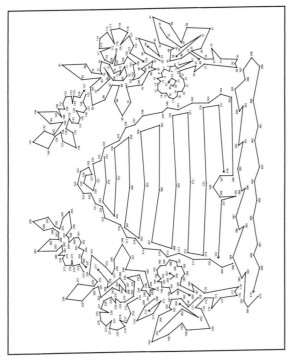

Puzzle 96

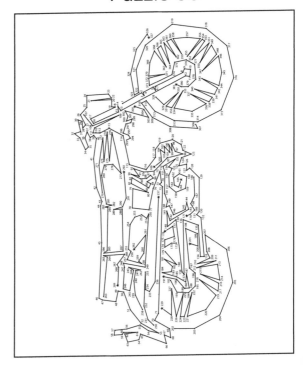

Puzzle 97

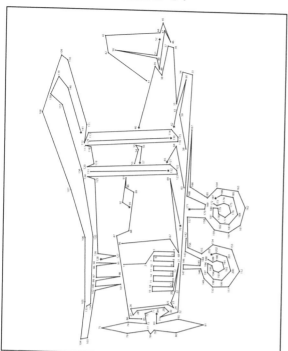

Puzzle 98

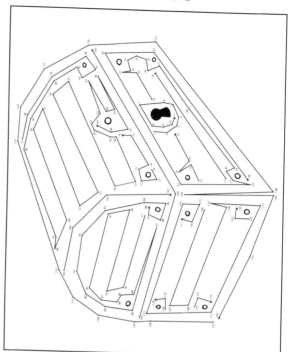

Puzzle 99

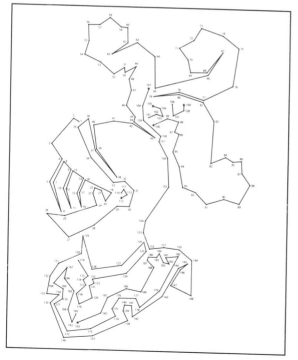

Puzzle 100

153

Puzzle 101

Puzzle 102

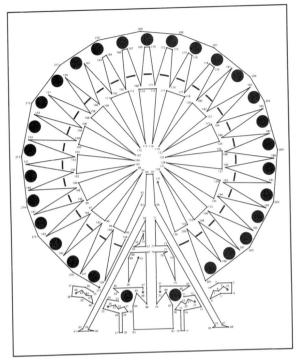

Puzzle 103

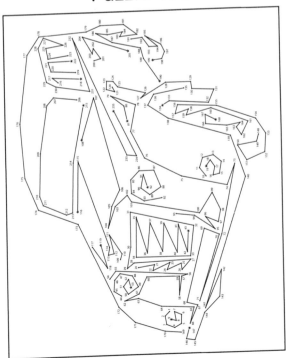

Puzzle 104

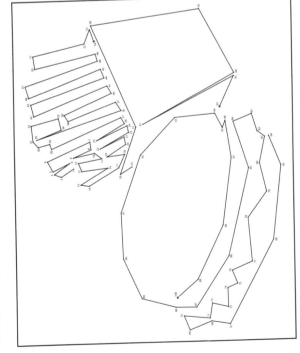

Puzzle 105

Puzzle 106

Puzzle 107

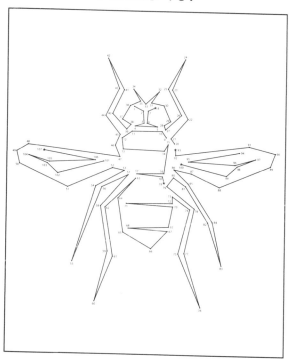

Puzzle 108

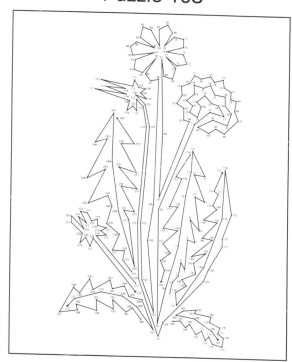

Puzzle 109

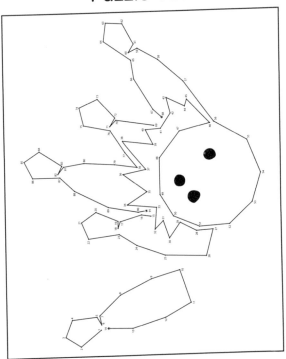

Puzzle 110

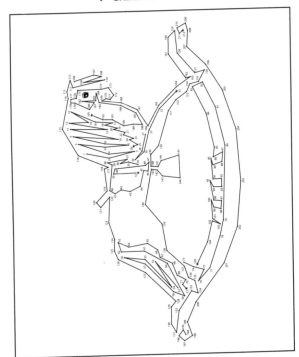

Puzzle 111

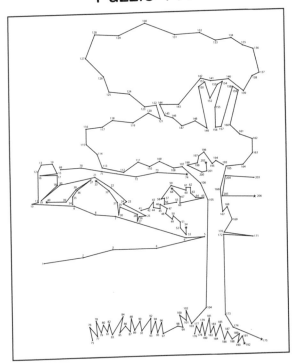

Puzzle 112

Puzzle 113

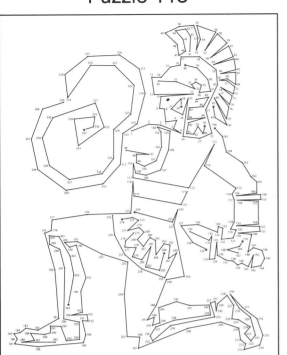

Puzzle 114

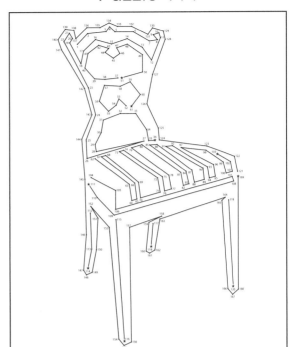

Puzzle 115

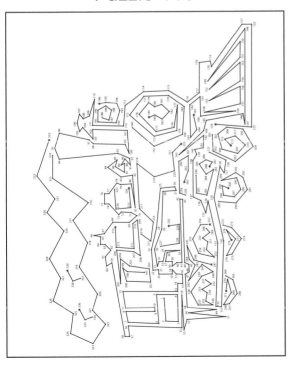

Puzzle 116

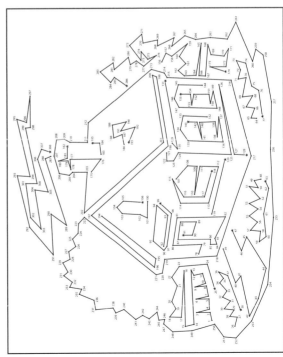

Puzzle 117

Puzzle 118

Puzzle 119

Puzzle 120

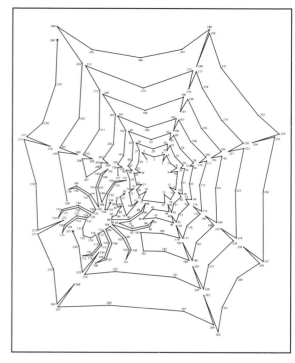

Puzzle 121

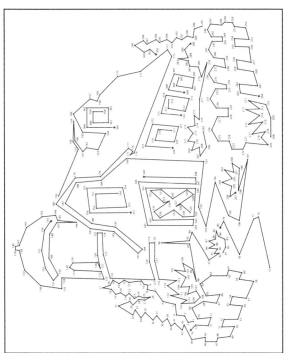

Puzzle 122

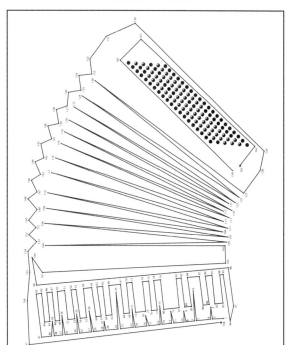

Puzzle 123

Puzzle 124

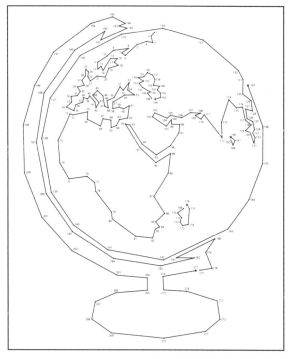

Puzzle 125

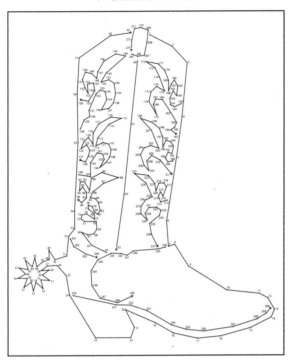